Sassy and Rude: Her New Attitude

Debra Mandel, Ph.D.

Sassy and Rude: Her New Attitude

A Tough-Love Guide for Moms on How to Bring Back The Sugar and Spice in Her Not-So-Nice Adult Daughters

Urano
publishing
Argentina - Chile - Colombia - Spain
USA - Mexico - Peru - Uruguay

8871 SW 129th Terrace Miami FL 33176 USA

Urano
publishing

Cover art and design by Luis Tinoco

The first edition of this book was published in December 2023

ISBN: 978-1-953027-24-5

E-ISBN: 978-1-953027-25-2

Printed in Spain

Library of Cataloging-in-Publication Data

Mandel, Debra

1. Personal Development   2. Relationships

Sassy and Rude: Her New Attitude

Dedication

I dedicate this book to all the mothers and daughters who have struggled to find peace and joy with one another, and especially to my deceased mother, Laine, and my beautiful daughter, Tiffany.

Mom-thank you for birthing and raising me! Your life was way too short. And while we didn't succeed in our efforts to overcome our struggles before you passed, I have always and will forever love you with all my heart. You laid the foundation for me to seek growth and healing despite adversity. I'm eternally grateful for you!

Tiffany-you are the greatest blessing in my life! Your effervescent spirit, exuberance, empathy, generosity, and wisdom shines light on me and everyone who encounters your kind and loving heart. I wouldn't trade a single moment throughout our relationship, even with all the tumult and pain. Each experience with you teaches me invaluable lessons, strengthens our bond, and gives me the confidence and momentum to strive toward even more depth of healing. Thank you for never giving up on me and continually calling on me to be a better person and mother. Of course, I also love the playful times. I adore you!

Acknowledgements

First and foremost, thank you from the depth of my heart to all the moms and daughters who have embraced me as their guide, sharing their tales, tears, triumphs, and defeats in their journey toward healing. These have not been easy struggles. Your candidness and bravery will continue to serve as inspiration for future mother-daughter relationships.

Tiffany-this book would not be possible if it weren't for your unrelenting perseverance toward helping us get to the core depth of healing. You have taught me so much! I wish I had been a better mom to you, but please know that I'll always keep trying to get it "right."

Mom (deceased) and stepmom, Dora—no two women could have been more different. Had you ever met, though, I believe you would have gleaned wisdom from one another and even shared a laugh or two about the trials and tribulations around motherhood. Mom-you encouraged me to be fiercely independent and to never give up on my dreams. Dora-you have modeled patience and grace to the nth degree, providing me greater inner calm. I'm grateful to you both.

Dad (deceased)-Our bond transcended all the many emotional battles we endured. Thank you for continually raising the bar higher, forever encouraging me to strive to be the best I can be. I'll always hold your strength and courage in my heart. I love you dearly and miss you immensely.

Christopher-my love, best friend, and a never-ending source of emotional support-you have my heart! Thank you for always seeing the hope in our future and inviting me to continually grow to become a better partner. You're my rock!

Linda, my agent -wow! What can I say? You're a woman I truly admire. Plus, you've stuck by me even when any sane mind would say my writing career was over. Thank you for keeping me on your backlist. Hopefully, this book will put me on the front list.

Lydia-what a treat to have an editor who is so kind and enthusiastic. I love your spirit and energy. Thank you for your praise and encouragement, and for seeing the value in bringing my message of hope to all mothers and daughters around the world!

And, to my family and dear friends—your flow of love and validation keeps me grounded and excited for the unfolding of each new chapter of my life.

My deepest gratitude to all of you!

Table of Contents

Introduction

You've probably heard the saying, "Sugar and spice and everything nice, that's what little girls are made of." Well, maybe for a moment or two during infancy when they're bathed, swaddled, and sound asleep—but certainly not a fitting description when it comes to contemporary moms and their experiences with their adult daughters. Quite frankly, it might be better stated as, "Sassy and rude, with a big attitude, that's what many of our girls are made of!" Honestly, many moms are tearing their hair out not knowing how, or if, they can ever have a mutually gratifying relationship with their adult daughters.

I don't say this only from my background of more than thirty years as a psychologist, specializing in mending wounded and broken relationships. More importantly, I am a mom of an adult daughter who I love and deeply adore. But our relationship has not always been riding on Easy Street. We've had to work hard to figure each other out and learn to navigate through our differences with compassion and a willingness to change. It's an ongoing process. And like it or not, as the parent, I saw it as my job to initiate positive progression by figuring out my part in our negative dynamic. So please know I can relate to your pain.

My Story

Before I elaborate further, here's a little of my own background prior to the insight that pushing her toward taking steps to make positive changes in her life would only lead to conflict between us. But her lack of self-care became so profound I finally decided, rather than remaining silent to avoid her wrath, I would proactively encourage my mother to change her path of self-destruction. Ultimately, I mustered up the courage to boldly suggest that she seek professional help. Not surprisingly, this did not go over well. Instead, my mother, in a fit of rage, blurted out the words, "Leave me alone! You are the worst daughter in the world!" Of course, I never would have thought that those would be the last words she ever spoke to me, let alone that she would no longer exist on this planet. As you can imagine, that was one of the most shocking and devastating experiences of my whole life. Sadly, I believe my mom passed away perceiving me to be *sassy and rude*.

When I was a young child, before I had developed my sense of self, I did everything possible to earn my mother's love and approval. I doted on her. I saved every penny from my allowance to buy her the perfect Mother's Day and birthday gifts. I pushed myself beyond perfectionism in school to bring home grades that would make her proud of me. When I got straight A's she and my dad would toss my report card aside and ask me why they weren't A+'s. I placated her interests, not that I had any other choice, by enduring seven years of piano lessons, learning only classical pieces, whereas my friends were learning to play musical instruments with hip, modern songs. Not that it was a bad thing. I did everything possible to earn my mother's love and approval before I developed my sense of self. My mother wanted me to be more cultured, but it would have been nice to have a little more fun while being forced to do something I had no interest in at the time. Maybe I wouldn't have such a love—hate relationship with my beautiful baby grand piano. To this day, it still sits in my living room begging me to dance my fingers across the keyboard while I go back and forth in my head with fear and intimidation that I'll make a mistake while playing a tune. While I certainly have more healing to do around the piano thing, I have recently made efforts to play some of the simpler pieces I once learned. Progress, not perfection.

No matter how hard I tried to please my mom, she just never seemed to like me. I guess I rubbed her the wrong way. In hindsight, I have a suspicion that my mom may not have truly wanted children, or certainly not at such a young age. Before meeting my dad, she enjoyed her independence through a successful career as a model, and I think that gave her a boost in her sense of self-worth. Nevertheless, as a child with limited ability to understand the root causes of other people's behavior, I could only accept that the harsh discipline she gave me was "for my own good" and because I deserved it.

When I look back now, I don't believe my mother hated me. Rather, I believe she truly loved me, but she was too wrapped up in her own disappointments in life. When she would have a few cocktails and let loose, a more tender heart would emerge, and I would catch a glimpse of the love buried in her heart. However, these moments weren't the norm and mostly I felt like I was unworthy of love. More commonly, she would scold me, tell me I was stupid, and judge me harshly for my curious mind. But nevertheless, because I so desperately wanted to feel her love, I never stopped trying to get her approval. In fact, I only tried harder, meanwhile feeling worse and worse about myself, crawling deeper and deeper into depression and despair. By adolescence, I turned a corner and sadly acted out my despair through an eating disorder, drugs, sex, and whatever means I could find to get love and approval from all the wrong people, in all the wrong places.

Fortunately, I had the wherewithal to work my way out of my funk and I took the path of becoming a psychologist, wherein I became engaged in learning the workings of the human mind and how emotional wounds trickle down from one generation to the next. I became aware that when emotional wounds remain unhealed, they cause us to recreate our pain in other significant relationships in an unconscious attempt to cultivate a different, more positive outcome. Yet, more times than not, the same dysfunction ensues until we become mindful and aware of our pain and what we need to heal it.

In my graduate program I found a great deal of love and support from my classmates, teachers, internship supervisors, and mentors. I began to open my eyes to the idea that maybe it wasn't all me who caused my mother to disdain me. I started to ponder that maybe I wasn't so bad after all. Maybe my mom had issues of her own. And, through the help of a therapist, I gained a deeper understanding of my mother's own personal, sad history and her fear of addressing the depth of her emotional wounds. I began to realize that I had been the scapegoat for my mom's unhappiness. Our relationship didn't stand a chance. It was no wonder we just couldn't get it right.

The more I was able to physically distance myself from my parents by living on my own, as well as increasingly gaining financial independence, the more I began to separate emotionally and find my own voice. I still heard a lot of toxic commentary from my mom, but I got more adept at letting the blows roll off my shoulders and was more able to refrain from diving too deeply into a pool of shame. I recall one time when I went for a visit to my folks' house my mother asked me, "WHAT have you done to your hair? It looks terrible!" At first, the blow felt like the sting of a hundred bees attacking all at once. But rather than react with tears and regret for my new hair style, I turned to my mom and said, "You can't talk to me that way anymore. I'm leaving." And I turned around and walked out the door. We didn't speak for three months. On other occasions, she would threaten to withdraw support for my graduate school if I didn't comply with her demands to get the program done quicker; a request with which I had no way to fulfil based on my school's curriculum. Examples such as these were many.

As I gained better and more polished coping skills, I spent less time trying to please my mom. Rather, I focused more of my energy on trying to heal from the pain I felt from the relationship with her so that I would minimize the chances of continuing the generational cycle of dysfunction. Of course, I wished I had had an opportunity to work things out with my mom, but I wasn't so fortunate. As you can imagine, it took years for me to recover from her sudden death almost thirty years ago and the prickling pain of the last words she'd spoken to me. To be perfectly honest, the deep sadness I felt about not having a close connection with my mom has never gone away entirely. Thankfully, for the most part I have found peace with it, and I cherish the deep love for her I hold in my heart.

Please know that I don't relay this story to inspire pity. I truly believe the relationship I had with my own mom was a blessing in disguise. Of course, I didn't come to that conclusion overnight. Rather, my understanding of my relationship with my mother took several years of psychotherapy and deep healing work that continues today. But the best thing of all was the day I became the mother of my beautiful and remarkable daughter, Tiffany. It was then that I truly knew that if I learned lessons from my experience, I would be better equipped to plant the seeds for a loving and nurturing relationship with her. After all, I would hate myself if my daughter were to ever feel unloved or unaccepted the way I felt with my mom.

Mind you, just like I'm not seeking pity, I am also not seeking endless praise. I just want you to know that there is hope. Also, I certainly made my fair share of mistakes as a parent and continue to do so. Nevertheless, my growing insights into the complications of a mother—daughter relationship motivated me to work as hard as I could to transform my pain into a healthy desire to nourish my relationship with Tiffany. Hence, the one promise I made to myself as a takeaway from my tragic relationship with my mom was to do everything in my power to have a wonderfully amazing relationship with my daughter. I don't really know if my mom suffered in her heart wondering why she and I were never close. I couldn't know because she wouldn't share her inner thoughts and feelings with me, aside from expressing anger. But I do assume that it made her sad on some deep level to have missed the chance at having a more enriched bond with me. And, I have certainly grown to understand from a mother's perspective the pain that comes from discord between a mother and daughter. Plus, I also grew to fully appreciate that if I was suffering, so too was my daughter. It is from this personal journey, along with my professional experience, that I came to write this book.

The Problem

Many baby-boomer moms, especially those like me who were raised by parents with a heavy hand or a spare the rod, spoil the child philosophy, brought up their little girls with endless love and adoration, showering them with gifts, praise, and undivided attention. All the while, these moms were hoping their daughters would appreciate how much "better" they were as mothers than their own moms had been. Unbeknownst to them, they may have even been seeking approval and validation from their daughters to make up for what they had so craved from their mothers. As a result, they inadvertently created a not-so-nice creature with very little sugar and spice. That's not to say that a gentle and kind mothering style lacks great value. Quite the contrary. However, if a nurturing style isn't coupled with self-awareness of unhealed emotional wounds, along with the ability to set clearly defined limits and boundaries, what can result is another wounded bird who appears with a greedy, it's all about me and my needs, posture. In essence, untamed entitlement runs amok, creating the too-nice mother/overly indulged daughter syndrome. And if the mom attempts to set any of these limits, these daughters may, in fact, perceive their mothers to be *sassy and rude*.

Apart from those moms who are severely narcissistic, and you're not one of them or you wouldn't have picked up this book, most modern moms not only desire, but actually crave, a good relationship with their daughters; and not just during the terrible twos through the teenage blues, but throughout the lifespan. In fact, one of the greatest hopes of today's moms is that someday after the passing of the tumultuous teens, they will develop a lifelong friendship with their grown daughters. Simultaneously, one of the greatest fears of many moms is that their adult daughters will kiss them goodbye as they leave the nest (with a smirk on their faces) and never look back, regardless of all the efforts made to give these young women every opportunity to succeed in life.

Fortunately, most moms and daughters don't become completely estranged as I had with my mom (unless there was severe abuse coupled with no accountability), and most continue a relationship to some degree. But tragically, these bonds are often horribly dysfunctional, fraught with constant battling, hurt feelings, angry outbursts, and unnecessary struggles for control. And, while our daughters certainly suffer, we mothers are often devastated beyond words because we have already invested so much of our time and energy without expecting much in return from our daughters while raising them. Or so we thought. Though, if we're being super honest, we'd probably have to admit that this investment is not entirely unconditional. Whether we like to acknowledge it or not, on some level we expect gratitude and appreciation once our daughters become adults. But unlike our mothers, who expected one-directional respect and loyalty, contemporary moms want gratitude and approval through a meaningful reciprocal relationship with their daughters. Without this bond, many moms feel a constant ache in their hearts and become mired in guilt and disappointment.

Also, today's moms have an even harder challenge to face than had their own moms (or even their grandmas) because many moms (in relation to their own mothers) tended to be extremely fearful of parental disapproval. They relied more heavily on the "blood is thicker than water" mentality, thereby being willing to put up with even the most blatant of abuse, if only to be able to keep the relationship intact. Today's adult daughters feel far more confident and independent and far less needy of approval from others, let alone from their mothers. They want and expect the freedom to make their own decisions without feeling any pressure to have to consult with mom. In many of the mother-daughter duos I've treated, the daughters didn't feel a strong loyalty to family, especially those who were not yet mothers themselves. Many actually appeared pretty self-centered and focused on their own goals seemingly without much, if any, concern for who they may hurt along the way. But, upon further digging, it became clear that their bark was often much worse than their bite; i.e., they did care, but they were hurting deep inside and just didn't feel safe to show it in ways that registered for mom.

If this resonates with you, please know that you are not alone. You, like so many other moms, may be recalling things your daughter has said to you in one of her "mean" moments like, "You've never supported me," "Get off my back," "Go get a life," or "I don't need you"— and all you can think about is every long-night conversation you had holding her hand, rubbing her forehead to ease her stress, consoling her through her first breakup, her fights with her best friend, her rejection from the college of her dreams, and every itemized checkbook entry/credit/debit card charge that went toward her ballet lessons, soccer team expenses, prom dress, etc. When those nasty moments occur between mother and daughter, it causes pain that pierces your heart worse than if you had discovered your intimate partner (or now ex) in bed with another woman, or if you've ever found out that your best friend is diagnosed with cancer, with no hope for recovery. It's a pain that permeates more deeply than the experience of having a root canal without Novocain. At least with the tooth scenario, you know that the pain will subside once the dentist turns off the drill.

Do you share this pain? If you answered yes—you are not alone. And don't despair. I've had hundreds of women pouring into my office heartbroken and devastated because they're embattled with their adult daughters, or their daughters won't even give them the time of day. It's bad enough if their daughters have moved out, but it's even worse when they're still, or back, living under the same roof. And since COVID-19, many adult children have needed to move back into their parent(s)' home for a variety of reasons. If the relationship between mother and daughter was already strained, this became a recipe for disaster.

So, what's a "too nice" mother to do?

The Solution

Clearly there are lots of books addressing the trials and tribulations of the mother—daughter relationship and each is filled with good advice.

But if you picked up this book, my guess is it's because you want help as a tender-loving mom to get you through the turbulent process of creating a healthy relationship with your "not so nice" daughter. And, by the way, your daughter probably thinks you're the one who is rude. If so, then you've come to the right place. *Sassy and Rude,* filled with examples and interviews from real-life mothers and daughters (including clients, friends, and relatives) anecdotes, exercises, and checklists, and combined with a tough love, yet compassionate tone, will provide you with the seeds to create a healing tree so you can:

- Connect the dots between your own childhood wounds and the ways in which you parented your daughter.
- Gain deeper insight into your daughter's wounded heart.
- Embark on a self-love healing journey.
- Stop power struggles once and for all.
- Face conflict and differences in a more constructive way.
- Accept responsibility for your own role in creating the rifts.
- Become able to finally find peace in your heart.

Sassy and Rude also addresses several very important questions we moms need to ask ourselves before we can embark on building the relationship we want with our adult daughters such as:

- Are my expectations unreasonable?
- What emotional wounds am I still carrying forward from my childhood and how have these affected my parenting style?
- Why aren't we close anymore?
- Why does she get angry every time I call/give her advice?
- Why is she so critical of me?

And although this book is aimed at *you* and your healing, you will also find a great deal written about what your daughter may be thinking and feeling. After all, your daughter may also be asking herself, "Why is my mother so rude?"

Most importantly, this book will enable you to become free from guilt and despair because you will learn that you can't control who or what your daughter becomes, while simultaneously developing the knowledge of how to put new and healthy ingredients into the relationship so that you can maximize the potential a healthier and more fulfilling bond. And, while there's no guarantee, hopefully your healing journey will also inspire your daughter to join in on this beautiful quest with you.

This book is fitting for mothers of adult daughters across the life span who:

- Have serious conflict with their adult daughters.
- Don't understand why.
- Are interested in taking responsibility for building a better relationship with them.
- May or may not have had a good relationship with them during the treacherous teens.
- Want a better relationship than they have had, or have, with their own moms.
- May also want to try to apply the content to her own role as an adult daughter with her own mother.

I know, this may all sound too good to be true. In fact, it wouldn't surprise me at all if you are at your wits end about how to mend your relationship with your daughter and/or are skeptical that anything will change, short of either you or your daughter getting a frontal lobotomy. But please, even if you think you've tried everything, maybe, just maybe, you'll find a seed that will turn things around.

Since you picked up this book, I'm encouraged that you are willing to recognize that the health and wellness of a relationship involves the ingredients put in by both parties. In other words, if your relationship isn't working with your daughter, then you probably recognize that you are likely part of the problem. Hence, that gives you the power to become part of the solution. You may not have a clue as to what role you might be playing in why your daughter snubs you, but at least you're willing to look at the whole picture, including your own responsibility. For this, I applaud you! It's far easier to point the finger at someone else and expect the other to make all the changes than to look in the mirror and ask yourself, "What am I doing to contribute to this issue?" So, good job on taking this next step.

As a side note, you'll find many "sugar and spice" exercises throughout the chapters. Some are aimed just at you, whereas others include contact with your daughter. Hence, depending upon the magnitude of distress between you and your daughter, especially if quite severe, you may want to hold off on practicing those exercises that involve her until you've read through all the chapters.

Most chapters were written to lay a foundation for the one that follows it, but you don't have to read them in sequence. If you're someone who likes to jump around, feel free. Just make sure you eventually capture each chapter as there may just be a small kernel of wisdom embedded where you least expect it, and I wouldn't want you to rush the process without sufficiently prepping the garden that will ultimately allow you to plant the seed for growing your healing tree.

CHAPTER 1

Carolyn's Story

Just as no two human beings ever turn out exactly alike (even identical twins), no two mother—daughter relationships overlap perfectly. And in the case of mother—daughter-duos-gone-awry, each mom has her own trials and tribulations that can at times make her feel as if no other mother on Earth could possibly understand the depth and uniqueness of her frustrations and challenges with her daughter. It's during those times a mom is likely to feel as if she is a creature from another planet, attempting to convey to an earthling what it's like to breathe without oxygen. But regardless of the unique nuances of each mother—daughter pair, most moms do share many commonalities. And, from my experience as a mom who has gone through her own despair about her relationship with her adult daughter, coupled with decades of hearing stories from other moms both personally and in a professional capacity, I think I can safely say that we moms may share more similarities than differences. Especially if you relate to being the "too-nice" mom.

As such, please know that whatever you've been going through, including both your agony and ecstasy of raising your daughter, you are not alone in your feelings and experiences. Thus, as you read on, even if I don't describe or provide an exact example relevant to your situation, try to extrapolate what's close enough to your story so you can find some comfort through a sense of belonging.

Like countless other moms, you have probably felt a myriad of emotions from sad to mad to scared when you think about how someone (that is, your precious daughter), whom you love so dearly, could turn into such an ungrateful, ornery, or even downright nasty human being. No doubt, you may have also run the gamut of feeling alone, hopeless, helpless, or certainly bewildered. Hey, you may have even felt crazy at times. "How could she be so mean to me and say such horrible things? I was the one who changed all those stinky diapers, who absorbed so many of her tears at all hours of the day and night when all I wanted to do was take a hot bath and run away from the world. I even listened to and often indulged those never-ending series of whims and desires presented as life-or-death scenarios!", you might think in fits of exacerbation.

After all, you cleaned up her vomit when she ate too much cake at her best friend's 4th birthday party, even though you told her that she would get sick if she consumed that much junk. Not to mention the countless times you rubbed her back, staying up all night singing her favorite nursery rhymes when she was a little girl suffering from a bad cold or was just too cranky to go to sleep. As she got older, you weathered all of her extracurricular activities, schlepping her from place to place so that she wouldn't miss out on any potential life experiences, even on those days when it was pouring rain and you just wanted to stay in bed with a cup of hot chocolate (maybe even spiked with your favorite liqueur) watching another episode of *Sex and the City*. (And probably wondering if you would ever even have sex again.) And at the end of the day, all you asked for in return was a loving hug before saying goodnight.

Once she hit those tumultuous teens, no doubt you bit your tongue countless times, refraining from passing judgment about the ridiculously unnecessary dramas your daughter became enmeshed in. You might have heard you own mother's voice in your head ushering you to tell your daughter to knock off her whiny nonsense or to stop making mountains out of molehills. But instead, you said something far gentler like, "Oh sweetie, sorry this is troubling you so much. I'm sure there will be a brighter light at the end of the tunnel." Why? Because you wanted to soothe and nurture her. Even when you clearly saw how disproportionate her response was to the actual event she was reacting to, you didn't want her to be embarrassed by her level of emotional drama.

You built up her self-esteem by incessantly complimenting her even when she would tell you how stupid you are and that you don't know or understand anything about adolescence. "Really," you would think to yourself. As if you just magically became an adult woman without ever passing through your own teenage crisis. Nevertheless, you did everything in your power to monitor your own impulsive reactions for the sake of never ever hurting your daughter's feelings. And like any mom, even those considered "too nice", you probably lost your shit on occasion and may have said some things you later regretted. Like me, you probably failed miserably at getting it all right, but most importantly, you tried your very best to do your part to help her feel special, loved, and wonderful.

Likely, you have/had sacrificed many of your own needs for your daughter to have more and better than you had in your life and who would feel cherished, possibly in a way that you never experienced with your own mom. You put off many of your own goals and aspirations so that you would make sure she never felt neglected. And if you were or are a working mom, you may have endured many sleepless nights with feelings of guilt, fearful that you weren't available enough for your little princess.

"And all for what?", you might be thinking. Now she treats you like you are expected to do all these things for her as if you owe her your whole life to ensure her happiness. As if you had agreed not only to become the bank account for automated bill pay, but also to serve as a punching bag for her never-ending frustrations and needs for emotional relief. Or possibly even worse, she ignores you or shuts you out from her life entirely.

Sure, at times she may say, "Thank you" or "It's ok, Mom, I can figure this out myself," when she sees you stressed out like a famished dog roaming about in an unfamiliar neighborhood. But often, as it turns out, many of these niceties were simply attempts to grease you with kindness for the next round of demands and entitlements. Wow! Talk about a thankless job. Nevertheless, while I can't say for certain, I would venture a strong guess that your daughter doesn't even perceive herself as sassy and rude. Even further, she probably doesn't even think you've been "too nice". Rather, she's probably wondering why you don't get how you've hurt her or disappointed her, and she just doesn't have the tools yet to navigate her own confusion and despair about the big black hole that the two of you have fallen into. But, if you're willing to start fresh with new behaviors, expectations, and attitudes, you *can* break this negative feedback loop and create a healthier and more fulfilling dynamic between the two of you.

Let's meet Carolyn again, keeping in mind that no example will be an exact replica of your unique relationship with your daughter. However, hopefully the following story about the destruction and repair of Carolyn's relationship with her daughter, Shelby, will have enough elements of commonality to your experience that it will give you hope and inspiration to jump onto a new path for transformation.

Carolyn's Story

Carolyn, a fifty-four-year-old homemaker-turned-interior designer, sought out my help while in utter desperation. Within seconds of the start of our session she exploded in tears. While she had mentioned when we spoke briefly on the phone to set an appointment that she was having problems with her daughter, clearly, she had minimized the impact her situation was having on her. Before she even said one word, I could see that she had not slept well for some time, and I could sense the heaviness in her heart as if she were lying on the ground with a fifty-pound weight on her chest.

Once I was able to help Carolyn soothe herself and calm her sobbing, she was able to find the words to share the specifics of her distress and she revealed a very sad, yet far too common, story. While once a vibrant, enthusiastic woman and a very proud mother, Carolyn had slowly and progressively deteriorated into a state of despair and hopelessness, fearing that she would never be able to have a warm and loving relationship with her now grown-up twenty-four-year-old daughter, Shelby. While Shelby would once have been described as a delightfully charming and gregarious young girl, now her mother could barely come up with any positive adjectives to attach to her. Carolyn shared that no matter what she tried to do to make things better with Shelby (e.g., taking her on a mother—daughter getaway, cooking her favorite meals, or trying to have a heart-to-heart talk with her), she and her daughter continued to bicker endlessly, with Carolyn constantly throwing up her arms in defeat while gasping for air as she cried uncontrollably while Shelby stormed out of the room in anger. "How could this happen to me and my daughter?", Carolyn would ask herself in utter desperation.

Carolyn was raised in a small town in the Midwest by two parents who struggled hard to keep food on the table and create a nice home for her and her two siblings, an older brother and younger sister. While Carolyn appreciated her parents for their efforts at providing for the family, she was not without resentments for many of the ways in which her parents treated her in her youth. There was no physical abuse per se, though some of the punishments she described would certainly raise eyebrows for the folks working at Child Protective Services if reported today. Rather, what pained Carolyn most was the lack of warmth and affection she longed for so deeply.

Carolyn described her mother, Mary, as stoic and reserved. According to Carolyn, if she came to her mom for a hug and reassurance when she was sad or afraid, Mary would quickly brush her away, insinuating that she should stop being so needy. Then Mary would talk about her own woes, expecting the empathy that she failed to provide for Carolyn. Her father, Jim, was a bit more playful and engaging but only when he was unstressed, which rarely occurred. More often, Jim was stern and detached. Carolyn clearly stood out as the sensitive one of the family, constantly seeking love and approval by being the good girl. That is, the girl who worked hard for good grades, followed the rules, and didn't make waves. But regardless of her efforts, she never quite got the gold stars she hoped for.

Carolyn often fantasized about one day having children of her own and being able to create a different experience than she had with her parents—that is, a parent—child relationship filled with joy, love, and closeness. Not that she could control the gender of her child, but she certainly dreamed that she would have at least one girl. While the hopes of fulfilling her future dreams helped to appease her lonely heart, she couldn't wait to leave home. At nineteen, after saving up enough money to get herself some wheels and move away from home, she made her way to Los Angeles, where she worked her way through community college. Sometimes she regretted moving so far from her family, but she truly felt there was no other choice if she were to stay sane. Fast forward a few years, while employed as a manager at a furniture store Carolyn met Dave, the man who would become her husband.

Carolyn and Dave fell in love and married when Carolyn was twenty-six. She was desperate to have children but for financial reasons they opted to wait a couple of years until they were more stable. When Carolyn was twenty-nine and Dave was thirty-five, they were able to conceive quickly, and Carolyn's ultimate dream came true—the birth of an adorable and healthy baby girl, whom they named Shelby. Carolyn, of course, could not have been happier. Sure, she would have been equally thrilled with a healthy baby boy, but the fact that she bore a daughter upon first try was a bit of a secret extra delight. Dave, a very loving and devoted husband and father, was solvent enough to enable Carolyn to be a stay-at-home mom without all the financial worries she knew her parents had endured.

For several years, it would be fair to say that Carolyn experienced what many people would label nirvana. Except for a few months of sleep deprivation and new-mom anxieties, Carolyn was happy, and her life revolved around creating a blissful life for Shelby. Mommy-and-me classes, planning tea parties, story-time, and snuggle-time filled her heart with joy. On occasion, Carolyn missed the workplace experience, but by and large, she loved her life. Dave and she had always planned on having two kids. When Shelby was three, they gave birth to their son, Todd. Naturally, life became more complicated when a sibling came into the mix, but all in all the family unit thrived for many years.

Once both kids were in grammar school, Carolyn got a little antsy with the extra time on her hands and decided to pursue a part-time career in interior design. She and Dave had the usual ups and downs in a marriage, but they generally worked things out without too many feathers ruffled. Carolyn loved spending time with her kids and especially enjoyed the mother—daughter closeness she had rarely felt with her own mom. Throughout middle school, and even the first few years of high school, Shelby loved hanging out with her mom, often even preferring to be with her mom over her friends. They played tennis, cooked delicious meals, and enjoyed shopping together. Shelby liked helping her mom pick out colors and fabrics for Carolyn's clients and Carolyn loved helping Shelby with her homework and nurturing her through her fears and worries. Certainly, Carolyn and Shelby had their share of quarrels, but nothing out of the ordinary and rarely ever to a level where they couldn't stand to be in each other's company.

Then, Shelby hit her sophomore year of high school and the shit hit the fan, so to speak. Based on Carolyn's description, the turn of events would be akin to watching a bomb explode in your living room and no longer recognizing any of the elements left in its wake, let alone being able to distinguish a sofa from a couch. Shelby no longer bore any resemblance to the sweet little girl whom everyone adored. Or at least when she related to her mom. Whereas historically Shelby had eagerly sought out guidance from Carolyn, now she rolled her eyes at everything her mom said. She became extremely rebellious and dismissive of any attempts Carolyn would make at setting rules or boundaries. She played her dad off her mom, creating fractures in their marriage. Meanwhile, thirteen-year-old Todd would try to step in to mediate between Carolyn and Shelby, but Shelby, who once adored her little brother, would call him hurtful names and/or completely ignore him as if he were an old worn-out Dr. Suess book tucked far beneath a pile of clothes in a garage storage bin.

To say the least, Carolyn was beside herself with anguish. In her eyes, she was losing her connection to Shelby, fearing that she and her daughter would end up estranged as she had with her parents—the very nightmare she'd worked so hard to not recreate. To make matters worse, because of not knowing how to fix their deteriorating relationship, Carolyn became more and more indulgent of her daughter, simply to avoid Shelby's wrath. Over time, Shelby became increasingly adept at exploiting her mother's weaknesses and manipulating her to get whatever she wanted.

Dave tried many times to point out this pattern, but Carolyn was not receptive to hearing criticisms and felt as if she were being ganged up on. Whenever Carolyn tried to set any kind of boundary, Shelby would become irate and forcefully wither her mother down to a sobbing mess. Shelby became more righteous, and Carolyn grew more depressed and hopeless.

Things improved ever so slightly when Shelby moved away to college, mostly because they naturally had more physical distance from one another and more time to breathe. But still, the negative-feedback loop had become so firmly entrenched that it seemed irreparable, and all they could each say about the other was, "Why is she such a BITCH?" Clearly, the rudeness factor was escalating.

Several more years passed, and Carolyn felt as if she'd gone through a death. She and Shelby rarely talked at all because their conversations became so unpleasant. Visits home for Shelby became fewer and farther between. And when they did occur, mother and daughter spent very little alone time together and mostly went through the formalities of being a family. Dave was clueless about how to intercede, and their marriage suffered. One day, when Dave came home from the office, he looked at Carolyn, and said, "I can't live like this anymore," implying that something needed to change, or he was out. And that's when Carolyn made the call to me and began her journey toward repair.

Our process together was quite grueling at times. In many ways, Carolyn was a woman who took on far too much responsibility for the problems and strain in the relationship with her daughter, and this allowed her daughter to bulldoze over her feelings. And because Carolyn was depleting herself of energy by investing all of it in trying to fix the relationship with Shelby, she inadvertently neglected the other important people around her; namely her husband and son.

When I first met Carolyn, I knew she needed compassion and nurturing. She certainly did not need to feel any worse about herself than she already felt. It was quite evident that she blamed herself for having "failed" as a mom. She did not demonstrate much capacity for self-love, but she certainly had far more than an adequate share of self-criticism coupled with tremendous self-loathing. She was excellent at caring for others, but relatively clueless about the importance of being attentive to her own needs. While Carolyn's sensitivity was certainly one of the most precious components of her as a person, she needed to build a thicker skin. She also needed to learn to fend off the inevitable blows likely to follow from her daughter once she attempted to hold her ground and set firm limits. She needed to become okay with the risk of having her daughter express hateful feelings toward her such as resentments, accusations, blame, disappointments, etc. Understandably, that was a terrifying concept to her. After all, what mother who loves her children would ever want to invite hatred from them? No one! Yet it was something she needed to accept as a possibility if she were to ever be able to change the dynamic.

Essentially, for Carolyn and Shelby to have a fighting chance, Carolyn needed to go through an internal transformation. She needed to become aware of how her own childhood wounds were still operative in her adult life, how these wounds played out in her parenting style, and how to accept what she had control over and what she didn't. She had to recognize that her continued over-indulgence of anyone would never tame the beast but would ultimately continue to give it fuel for its fire. That's not to say that Shelby was a beast. Quite the contrary. Shelby was well-liked by most people and quite popular. She had always gotten good grades and her teachers mostly reported that she was a pleasure to have in class. She performed well at her job as an account manager. She had solid friendships and even demonstrated more than average compassion and empathy toward others—just no longer toward her mom. Why? Shelby felt her mom didn't get her at all and that her mom never truly listened to her. Instead, her mom placed a Pollyanna spin on their conversations, leaving Shelby feeling misunderstood.

Carolyn also needed to heal from guilt and embrace the reality that setting boundaries does not equate to being a bad or unloving mother. She needed to accept that having raised her daughter in a manner that was almost the polar opposite of how her parents had treated her had ironically created its own set of problems, including wounds in her daughter's heart. She needed to face her own imperfections and make amends both for herself and her daughter. Of course, she had to gain these insights without blaming or shaming herself, which was no easy task.

Nevertheless, Carolyn willingly stepped up to the challenging journey of transforming herself, and ultimately her relationship with her daughter. She worked hard at letting go of the need for her daughter's approval and, over time, Carolyn learned how to cut things off at the pass before they would even have a chance of heating up. For instance, when Shelby would call Carolyn to ask (or rather, demand) that her mother help her with something she (Shelby) had neglected, Carolyn learned to say a version of one of my favorite boundary-setting practices. "Hi Shelby. I'm so glad to hear from you. I appreciate your confidence in my ability to handle this problem for you, but quite frankly I'm rather busy right now and your emergency isn't mine. I love you though and I trust you will be able to fix the situation yourself. If you'd like to have more discussions about this or would like my input, I would be available at...." It's kind of a gentle, yet firm, way of deflecting a conflict.

Of course, when Carolyn initially attempted this rather unnatural type of dialogue with Shelby, she bumbled around for a while and was easily manipulated back into her "too nice" mode, especially when Shelby would say hurtful things like, "You're so selfish, Mom!" Ouch! That's the last descriptive Carolyn could ever be accused of. "But if my daughter said it, then it must be true," Carolyn would think and believe. But Carolyn kept practicing setting her boundaries and she saw noticeable improvements in how she felt after her interactions with Shelby. She felt better and better even when Shelby would still act sassy.

Eventually, Shelby began taking to heart the many disclosures her mom had made to her about her own wounded heart and how these emotional bruises affected Shelby, both positively and negatively. Shelby also began noticing positive changes in her mother and grew to have more respect for her. She observed her mom taking better care of herself like working out at the gym, spending more time with her friends, and building new hobbies. Carolyn also learned the art of active listening and giving up the need to tie a pretty bow around every conversation.

For a brief while, I was able to work with both mother and daughter, and not surprisingly discovered that Shelby also suffered great distress about the poor relationship she had with her mom. She often found her mom to be sarcastic and felt criticized by her indirectly. For instance, Carolyn occasionally would say something negative about a characteristic of one of Shelby's close friends, not realizing that Shelby perceived herself as having a similar quality. Hence, Shelby felt as if her mother had just put her down.

Because Shelby had a much tougher exterior than her mom, she didn't wear her sadness on her sleeve. But that didn't mean she didn't harbor hurt feelings. Fortunately, over time and with many modifications in the way they interacted with one another, they grew to find the fondness they had once felt so deeply for one another. For instance, they made an agreement that either one of them could call a timeout on a conversation if it began to get heated and then choose an alternative time to pick up where they left off from a more centered space. They also took a meditation class together. Mind you, the love had never died, but it had become deeply buried beneath layers of hurt and resentment.

Carolyn and Shelby's relationship certainly wasn't perfect—whatever that would mean, anyway. They continued to have their ups and downs and periods of falling back into old patterns. Nevertheless, they both stayed motivated to push through the down times and keep making progress. Fast forward to a recent contact I had with Carolyn where I learned of a very positive outcome. Shelby had married and given birth to a daughter of her own. And guess who she invited to come stay with her and help out with her newborn? Yup—her mom!

What Lies Ahead

Of course, not everyone is as fortunate as Carolyn to have the resources to seek professional counseling. And there is no guarantee that you, or any mom, will have the same positive result as Carolyn and Shelby. But I'm confident that if you go through the remaining chapters, apply principles, and practice the exercises, you can make positive changes and will see improvement in your relationships overall; especially the relationship you have with yourself. Ideally, your daughter will become more attracted to your energy and will want some of whatever you've been having. She'll see that she doesn't have such power in making you feel bad, and she will likely change. Preferably, for the better. Anyway, at this point whatever you've been trying hasn't been working, so let's see if a different approach has a different and better result.

In the next chapter, I guide you through a self-love lesson so you can more accurately assess what is truly your part in this problem and what lies outside of your responsibility. If you're like Carolyn, you'll need a hefty dose of de-shaming and de-guilting yourself so that you can build the inner strength necessary to begin to make lasting changes. Please read on, thinking of me as your coach. If anything sounds critical or judgmental on my part, please know that my intentions are only to try to help you see another perspective, not to make you feel bad about yourself or about your parenting. Also remember, I've been in your shoes, at least to some degree, so I hope you can believe that I understand your pain. Sometimes we just need a good reality check to jolt us out of stagnation and despair and back into hopefulness. So, when you're ready, go ahead and turn the page and let's see if we can't bring back some sugar and spice in your not-so-nice adult daughter.

CHAPTER 2

Is It Me or Is It She?

If you're like many moms, you've probably asked yourself the following questions: "Who's to blame? Is it me or is it she?" Or maybe even, "Why is she so rude to me?" You may have even thought, "Why is she such a bitch?" Of course, these questions are completely understandable given that so many of us were raised to believe that we must find the guilty party, i.e., someone to blame. All you have to do is see the headline of any news article and you'll be directed to focus on someone's guilt or innocence. While of course, in true crime situations we want to determine who is at fault, in most life situations, particularly with regards to the underpinnings of relationships, nothing is ever that black or white.

So, instead of perpetuating the blame—guilt—shame game, I encourage you right here and right now to throw out the notion of finding fault and instead look at your relationship with your daughter from a dynamic model. If you've heard the statement, "It takes two to tango", often used to describe relationships, then you'll understand what I'm saying. If not, then think of it this way: your relationship is like two people learning a new dance together that continually needs fine-tuning in its choreography. Whether it comes together smoothly depends on the dancers' skill sets, level of practice, history of dance, etc. Each partner's move affects the other. Hence, I encourage you to look at your part in the dynamic as honestly as possible and ultimately encourage your dance partner (your daughter) to do the same.

Sugar and Spice Exercise: Self-love

Before we go any further, let's pause in this moment for a little self-lovin'. After all, you have embarked on quite the journey here, and you'll need to be as grounded and centered as possible. When convenient, please find a comfortable and safe place where you can close your eyes and relax. I'd like you to then take five or six deep inhalations and exhalations, imaging yourself to be tranquil and strong. Next, give yourself a tender embrace and tell yourself, "No matter the mistakes my parents/caregivers made in raising me, the mistakes I may have made in raising my daughter, or mistakes she believes I've made, I did my best as a parent with whatever resources were available to me. Even if she is angry with me, I meant well and deserve forgiveness; if not from my daughter, then certainly from myself. I will continue to do my own healing in the process and keep my heart open. I'm worthy of love!"

The most important piece to this exercise is to penetrate your own shame or guilt and simultaneously begin to help you rid yourself of any anger or resentment toward your daughter. There will be much more to follow regarding these dynamics as you read on throughout the book. Now let's forge ahead.

Assessing Responsibility

You might be asking; how do we assess responsibility in a way to ultimately take charge of creating the best version of ourselves in relation to our grown daughters? First, we must become cognizant of our locus of control (i.e., where we have control versus where we don't), and secondly, we need to learn to accept the limitations of our capacity to control anything other than our own behavior. That's not to say that we don't have strong influence at times over those whom we love, but that's not the same as having control over them.

Before we launch into understanding the areas over which we have control, let's take a closer look at what it's like to be a child with a few real-life examples. As children, particularly during our first decade or so, we have been given virtually no choice over most aspects of our lives. Our parents or other influential caregivers such as teachers, aunts, uncles, grandparents, etc., have the power to call all the shots. They are in charge and ultimately responsible for our health and well-being while we are under their care. They tell us how to dress, how to hold a fork and knife, where to put our clothes, what and how to eat, what we can watch on television, and how much or what social media we can access. They guide our thinking, and they shape how we ultimately end up perceiving the world and the people in it. The list goes on and on.

As children, we also must contend with rules. Not our own rules, but the ones our caregivers design for us and tell us we must follow. In most good-natured families, rules are created primarily to keep us safe from harm. For instance, we might be asked to hold a parent's hand while crossing a busy street which is definitely a good safety practice. However, sometimes these rules are created by our caregivers to provide themselves with their own personal comfort and control, having little to do with creating safety and well-being in their children. For instance, we might be asked to be quiet in the morning so a tired parent can enjoy more sleep, even though we would love to laugh out loud as we see the neighbor's cat unsuccessfully try to hunt a robin taunting it from the oak tree in our yard. Certainly, our squeals of delight would not constitute any sort of danger. Rather, the rule is in place simply to keep mom or dad happy.

We may not like the rules and/or they don't make sense to us. But still, we are told we must follow them. Often, as we get a little older, the rules change to reflect the different life experiences we'll likely encounter during the developmental span of childhood. For instance, when you're five years old you may not be allowed to play with a friend without supervision, whereas you will probably be granted that permission later, once you've demonstrated good judgment and have reached an older age. Then again, that very rule might change again once you're a teenager with raging hormones, as your caregiver(s) worry about premature sexual exploration, resulting in becoming stricter yet again. These changes may confuse children, yielding difficulty in fully embracing the necessity for rules until we are much older, possibly not even until we have children of our own.

Then, of course, there is the issue of, "What happens when we break the rules?" Much of the time, we receive some sort of consequence. In some families, caregivers are more lenient than others (e.g., they reiterate the rule and move on) whereas others are a bit stricter (e.g., they take away our privileges). And still others can be downright abusive, leading to name calling, shaming, hitting, threatening abandonment, etc., none of which is good.

Imposing consequences generally aims to teach children about responsibility and possibly even about morals and values. For instance, if a child throws her toy at her sibling, a parent who wants her child to grow up with kindness as a value may take the toy away and impose a time out. Or a parent who wants her child to value honesty may restrict a child from playing on her iPad if she told a fib. Of course, as you probably already know, how caregivers teach these lessons varies considerably across families. While some of their methods can be very loving and clear, others can be quite dysfunctional and ineffective. Even with the more relatively benign family dysfunction, most children likely received confusing messages regarding where control and responsibility start and stop. Hopefully you did not have any sort of physical or mental abuse, neglect, or abandonment, but if so, then the process of sorting out what you are responsible for is considerably more challenging. You may suffer from significant trauma and may need to do extra work on healing yourself. If that's the case, please use this book as a stepping-stone in the healing process while simultaneously seeking additional resources beyond the scope of this book. You are worth the time and energy necessary to clear a path to greater healing.

For further clarity, let's look at Lisa's story. Lisa, a forty-six-year-old mother of two daughters, was raised by parents who rarely took responsibility for themselves and who were caught in the throes of the blame—shame game. Her parents, Joel and Kathy, would bicker back and forth about trivial things, each blaming the other for their feelings, actions, and reactions. Joel would get angry at Kathy, she would snap back, and then he would yell and slam doors, telling Kathy that she was the cause of his aggressive behavior. Neither one felt understood by the other and usually they would brush things under the carpet until the next round of verbal combat, never getting any resolution. Their problem? Neither understood that they weren't responsible for the other's behavior or feelings. Yes, their own behavior influenced the other's behavior but that's not the same as causing it. Ultimately, Joel needed to take responsibility for his temper and Kathy for her snide remarks. Unlike when they were children and their own caregivers had dominant control over their lives, as adults, both of them had alternate options for how to handle upsetting situations. Yet, because neither of them had this awareness, they weren't able to move beyond their habitual, negative, patterns.

Naturally, Lisa observed their unhealthy dynamic and internalized the message that other people were responsible for her behavior and feelings. To make matters worse, both of her parents would blame Lisa for their upset with her. Her dad would say things like, "You're making me so mad", in reaction to Lisa having not put her clean clothes away in her drawers. Her mother might say, "You need to put a sweater on", when her mother perceived the temperature outside as chilly enough to warrant a coverup, even though Lisa would protest, telling her mom that she wasn't cold.

You might look at these examples and say, "What's the big deal?" Lisa didn't put her clothes away when she was supposed to. Of course, her dad got angry. Or her mom was just being a caring parent who didn't want her daughter to get cold or, worse yet, get sick. And you're right! Her parents did, in fact, have good and loving intentions, ultimately wanting Lisa to grow up to be a healthy and responsible young woman. But what may not be so obvious it that they were setting Lisa up to believe that she was responsible for other people's reactions and behaviors and ultimately to also believe that other people "made" her feel and act in certain ways, thereby clouding the lines of control and responsibility.

In the ideal world, Joel would have been able to identify that his anger grew out of his own expectations and that these expectations weren't necessarily reasonable to impose on a young child. By the way, Lisa was only five when tasked to clean up her room. Clearly good training for future organizational skills but kind of a stretch to expect such a young child to consistently follow that directive. Joel saw his daughter as being defiant and he believed he should assert greater control and hence chose to allow anger to rule his emotions. I'm not saying this wouldn't be a common response for many parents, but the bottom line is that Lisa did not "make" her dad mad. Rather, her dad, from his own interpretation of events and motives, became mad instead of "choosing" to be understanding and compassionate.

Kathy also unknowingly blurred the boundaries of control and responsibility by indirectly sending Lisa the message that Lisa didn't know her own body temperature and comfort level and would have to rely on the judgments of others to decide what to wear in varying climates. While using her own body temperature as the gauge for Lisa's, she made a projection about what Lisa needed. Parents do this all the time. But it can really mess with a young child's developing sense of reality and judgment. Again, in the hypothetically perfect world, Kathy would have instead said something like, "Sweetie, I'm going to have you bring a sweater with you, just in case you get cold." If Kathy needs a sweater for herself, she's more than welcome to take one. As it turns out, Kathy was simply passing along the same "caring" messages she received from her own mom.

While Lisa grew up to be a wife, mother, and successful small business owner in charge of several employees, she secretly lacked confidence in herself and her decision-making process. While others around her saw her as highly competent and capable, deep within herself she struggled with a lot of anxiety and doubt. And, because she hadn't connected the dots between her childhood struggles and her inner turmoil, she didn't recognize that her emotional wounds informed much of her own parenting style. And it wasn't until her twenty-four-year-old daughter, Teresa, completely snapped at her, calling her a stupid idiot that Lisa woke up to an awareness she hadn't really seen until then. It hit her like a ton of bricks that her daughter's growing resentment toward her stemmed from her own unresolved childhood confusion about control and responsibility. Unbeknownst to Lisa, she had given her daughter the same confusing messages her parents had given her. However, unlike Lisa, who turned this confusion into self-doubt, Teresa rebelled by taking a stance against her mom. Teresa didn't really think her mom was an idiot. Rather, she just wanted her mom to stop being so wishy washy.

Lisa didn't blame her parents for her own shortcomings. Rather, she was able to turn their mistakes into lessons about herself and opportunities to evolve into a better parent.

Understanding Control

"I don't want to be controlling," you might be thinking. Of course not. But the reality is that all of us must become aware of the things and the people we have control over and things and people we can't in order to break the chains of generational and relational dysfunction. In Lisa's situation, she felt so responsible for other people's feelings that she became a people-pleaser, yet simultaneously also acted somewhat like a victim because she also believed other people controlled her emotions. For instance, if a friend told her that she didn't like something Lisa had said, Lisa interpreted that to mean that her friend was trying to make her feel bad about herself. She didn't realize that her friend was just sharing her own experience.

I get it that the word control may conjure up a lot of negative associations because we often use this word to imply being a power mongrel, a control freak, someone who thwarts other people's freedom, or a manipulator. But for our purposes, I use the word in reference to our ability to self-regulate; i.e., to be responsible for our own actions, thoughts, and feelings. Granted, as I've mentioned, we do have influence over one another and we must take that into account, particularly when there is a power differential between individuals. For example, maybe you have, at some time in your life, felt controlled by a boss. But, in reality, your boss has never actually had control over you, since you always have the option to quit your job. However, that doesn't mean that if he or she had asked you to complete a task that you would not do it. Why? Because you want to keep your job! You're not being controlled per se, even though the directive highly informs the choice you'll make about completing the task. Of course, the situation becomes more complicated if you need your job and there aren't a lot of other options. But regardless, you're not being controlled. This may seem like I'm being petty or parsing words—but this concept is very important and intimately related to healing emotional hurts in our relationships with others. And right now, you want every tool you can find to help the sadness, anger, or myriad of other emotions you feel with regards to your bond with your daughter. So, the point is that unless you're truly being victimized in a situation (e.g., a gun pointed to your head) or you oversee the well-being of a dependent person, you're in control of only yourself and, hence, you're solely responsible for your own actions, feelings, and thoughts.

How is responsibility and control related, you might wonder. Very simply answered, we are responsible for that which we can control. No more, no less. In the real world, when we perceive something, we then interpret what we've observed, and then our emotions occur. Any actions I take as a result of my feelings become my responsibility. No one made me do it; only me. Hence, no one is responsible for your feelings except yourself. Granted, others do have influence over how we feel but we are ultimately the ones in charge. So, as adults, unless we are completely at the mercy of someone else (due to disability, mental illness, a hostage situation, etc.), we oversee ourselves. And the adults around us are also in charge and responsible for themselves. So, in approaching the healing with your adult daughter, keep in mind that you are no longer liable for her well-being or her choices. Nor has *she* ever been or will be in control of *your* choices! This may sound harsh, but it's not meant to be. Rather, it's meant to clear up the confusion about responsibility and control once and for all. Just like your computer cannot function properly if infected by a virus, nor can your relationship with your daughter become harmonious if colored by misguided ideas of who's responsible for whom or what.

Special note: You were highly influential in how your daughter became the person she is today, but now that she is an adult you don't have control over her anymore and she is ultimately responsible for her own actions. If your daughter is new to adulthood, then you might wish to cut her a bit more slack since she's in the transition stage to adulthood. If that's the case, I will ask you to still bear the lion's share of responsibility to get the relationship on a more positive track. Nevertheless, she still bears the burden of being responsible for her own actions and choices depending upon her level of independence from you.

Now, let's practice with an exercise.

Sugar and Spice Exercise: The Convo-Redo

Using the model outlined above, I suggest you take a few recent scenarios that haven't gone well with your daughter and try what I call a "convo-redo." Quite simply, it's trying to have a previous conversation that may not have gone the way you'd hope with new perspective, orientation, and tools.

(Daughter's Name): (Time Frame): (I observed…) (I interpreted that to mean) and then (I felt…) (Invitation to respond)

Example: "Hey sweetie, last week when we had our weekly chat on the phone, it seemed that you were in a hurry and not very present on the call. I was telling you about a lunch date I had with my friend, Jane, (who you love and adore) and you made a few comments that sounded sarcastic to me. I should have said something at the time, but I didn't because it hadn't really hit me until we hung up that I thought you might be upset with me about something or that maybe something was going on with you that you didn't feel you could share with me. In any case, I left our conversation feeling sad and disconnected from you. Of course, that was totally based on my own assumptions! I'd love to know more about your experience and to talk more about this when you get a chance. Please call me. Love you!"

There is no telling how "sweetie" will respond to this comment and invitation to address it, but at least it's a very clean communication. She could get defensive and say something like, "I have no idea what you're talking about," or "Why are you always reading into things?" If so, just take a deep breath and let her know that you aren't criticizing her or even stating that your observation or interpretation is accurate. You're simply sharing how you derived your feelings and asking if she'd like to fill in the gaps. She might also be thrown off guard and not trust this new you, especially if you haven't spoken to her like this previously.

Anyway, practice going through a few scenarios and if you feel brave enough to test the waters with her—go ahead. Or you might choose to hold off for a while and do the actual real-life practice once you get more tools up your sleeve. For now, mostly focus on becoming crystal clear in owning that which is your responsibility—again, nothing more, nothing less!

Okay, so now we've covered understanding control and responsibility. Hopefully, you have new insights to carry forward in understanding the dirty word of "manipulation."

CHAPTER 3

Mommy Sweetest to Mommy Meanest

At the risk of aging myself (But, who cares. It's just a number anyway.), back in 1981, the movie, *Mommie Dearest*, based on a book by Christina Crawford about her mother, Joan Crawford, was released. Ms. Crawford, played by Faye Dunaway, was characterized as an abusive and highly manipulative mother. In the portrayal, the mother was not only frightening, but downright cruel to her two adopted children (a girl and a boy). I remember watching it while working out on an exercise trampoline. In one scene in particular the mother was so mean toward her daughter, I became so upset that I forgot I was on the trampoline and ended up crashing down on the side of my ankle and broke it! To this day, I can visualize that scene as if I'd just watched it and recall how sad I felt for the young girl.

While I can't imagine you bear any resemblance to the mother characterized in the movie, I'm thinking this depiction resonates with you in some way. Possibly from the daughter's perspective. If you identify as a "too nice" mom, I suspect you might have had a mother who was also mean to you (or some other caregiver who may have mistreated you) and you vowed never, ever, to treat your own children with anything other than utter kindness. You suffered emotional scarring, and you were not going to pass this along to the next generation. However, I also suspect that if you didn't go on a conscious therapeutic journey to heal your wounded inner child, you may have inadvertently developed some coping mechanisms that affected your parenting style and that may ultimately have backfired. In other words, despite all your efforts to not recreate the same wounds in your daughter that you endured, you may have left behind other wounds, leading your own daughter to have grown to perceive you not as "mommy sweetest" but more like "mommy meanest." Again, this is not a blame or fault-finding mission. Rather, just the opportunity to possibly adopt a new perspective for understanding what went awry in your relationship with her, and to ultimately develop new tools and resources on how to once again become "mommy sweetest" in her eyes (i.e., bringing back your own sugar and spice). And this time around, you'll be equipped with better boundaries, a healthier voice, and more realistic expectations of yourself and of your daughter.

By the way, I don't mean to be too presumptuous about how a rift was created between you and your adult daughter. There are most likely countless explanations for how, or why, that occurred. But regardless of the specifics, you can still find healing by simply understanding yourself more clearly, and by compassionately letting go of that which you can't control. If nothing else, wouldn't you at least like to be free of your anguish and despair, even if you and your daughter don't yet have the harmonious relationship you desire? If you answered yes, then just like in the previous chapter where you placed a mirror in front of yourself to understand your responsibility, here we are going to look at the subtle ways in which we as moms may have inadvertently set ourselves up for negativity with our daughters by better understanding the word "manipulation."

What is Manipulation?

Let's face it; the concept of even remotely engaging in the process of manipulation is appalling to most of us. After all, in our culture "manipulation" has a very bad rap. It's a characteristic and behavior often associated with sociopaths, narcissists, and other less than desirable sorts of people. Yikes! Who wants to be put on that continuum of pathology? For most of us warm-hearted, generous, and loving souls, if we're ever accused of being manipulative, most of us cringe and drop into a shame hole. Or, alternatively, we fiercely defend against such a vile descriptor of ourselves akin to a chihuahua facing a frothy-mouthed pitbull who hasn't yet eaten breakfast.

Nevertheless, despite the negative connotation we have with the word, the act of manipulation has survival value and can be extraordinarily adaptive in nature. Well, at least in certain situations. And no doubt, whether you'd like to admit it or not, you've also learned to be manipulative; as has your daughter. However, the key to interrupting manipulative patterns is to learn to distinguish when it's adaptive and when it's harmful.

By the way, I'm joking when I refer to "manipulation" as a dirty word. As noted above, the act of manipulation can enhance our survival capacity. But it's extremely important to understand why we succumb to this tactic (conscious or unconscious) and how to break free from its hold.

Let's look at the true definition of the word. According to Merriam-Webster's dictionary online, to manipulate (verb) means to:

- "Treat or operate with or as if with the hands or by mechanical means especially in a skillful manner
- To manage or utilize skillfully
- To control or play upon by artful, unfair, or insidious means especially to one's own advantage

- To change by artful or unfair means so as to serve one's purpose."

With regards to its synonyms, Oxford Dictionary (online) lists:

- "Operate, handle, work, control, use, employ
- Or influence, maneuver, direct, guide, orchestrate, choreograph."

Clearly some of these definitions and synonyms aren't so flattering, but several of them convey great functionality and positivity such as: guide, choreograph, influence (if well-meaning), etc. In reality, it's all about context, whether its adaptive or maladaptive, and even possibly harmful.

Imagine being a young child primarily raised by a single mom whose ex is a deadbeat dad (e.g., fails to fulfill child support agreements, doesn't show up for important events, abandons emotional responsibilities, etc. The mom works overtime and barely gets by, fighting for her and her child's survival. Often, she's overwhelmed. Naturally, despite the mom's situation and exhaustion, her child needs ongoing care and attention because the child cannot yet fend for herself. Hence, the child must act to ensure her survival.

This child (let's say four years old) wakes up hungry and mom is still sleeping. It's already 8:30 am and the child has been up since 7:00 am. She's tired of playing with her toys. She tries many clever tactics, making loud noises, and ultimately gets her mother to wake up. But much to her dismay, her mother becomes angry with her. Hence, she must go back to the drawing board. Ultimately, without much conscious decision—making, she figures out through trial and error that if she wakes her mother by telling her she has a stomachache or some other physical ailment, her mother sympathizes with her, gets out of bed, and pulls it together just enough to take care of her child's belly ache.

No doubt the child "manipulated" her mother for her own purposes, yet no one would fault her. She didn't have many choices available. She couldn't say, "Mom, you know if you can't take care of me, I'm going to have to find another mother." Nor could she rely on herself—she wasn't yet capable. The child feared abandonment and was simply trying to survive. She needed her mother to get her breakfast. Hence, she created a story to get her mother's attention. The goal wasn't to hurt her mother. She wasn't even conscious of her actions. She was simply behaving in the most adaptive way available to her to preserve her own life.

While we may more easily empathize with a child who resorts to manipulation than an adult, it's important to recognize all of us, young or old, poor or rich, single or married, manipulate to some degree believing it will enhance our survival across the lifespan. For instance, with the example above, when that same four-year-old becomes an adult daughter, she might claim, or even develop, physical ailments every time her mom invites her to an event she doesn't want to attend. And, while she may still link that to her survival, that behavior prevents her from thriving. Hence, the key is to learn how to minimize the tendency toward manipulation when it's not necessary, i.e., when our survival doesn't require it. While it may be perceived as necessary, more times than not we are perceiving some level of danger when there is none. So, we don't recognize an option to enter by way of the front door in many situations. Instead, we find clever, sneaky, back door alternatives. Even well-meaning people will cross this line on occasion, especially if we haven't healed our inner child. In other words, if we still have unresolved emotional pain from our childhood, this can wreak havoc in all areas of our lives, at any point in time, with anyone, without our conscious awareness. We will behave in dysfunctional ways; namely through manipulative behavior.

Distinguishing Constructive Versus Destructive Manipulation

Using my definition, *constructive* manipulation is an attempt to persuade or influence another person that is relatively harmless to a person, has been consciously determined to be the best course of action based on the circumstances at hand, has at least some level of good intention behind it, or is trying to help someone feel good even though it may also be serving our own needs (needing to be liked, to receive approval, to reduce our guilt, etc.). Here are a few examples with your daughter:

- You make up a white lie because you are throwing her a surprise party.
- You give her flowers after her kitty cat just passed. You are actually intending to influence her to feel better *and* you may also want her to perceive you as extra caring because she was snippy toward you the last several months.
- You compliment her on a new outfit and tell her she looks good, even though you may not think it's the most flattering choice. After all, she just gave birth to your first grandbaby.
- You make up a benign excuse to decline her invitation to a dinner party she's hosting because you'd rather stay at home watching Netflix and eating popcorn with your hubby after three weeks of grueling work-related extra responsibilities.
- You entice her with a paid roundtrip ticket home, not for the holidays, but because you want her to help you through a rough patch in your life, and you sell it to her as a break from her routine. You know you should have told her the truth, but you sell it to yourself that it would be better to tell her once she is in your physical presence.

Please note that in all these examples, even though you can rationalize your actions as attempts to help facilitate positive feelings in your daughter or even prevent negative ones, you are still being somewhat self-serving. You are also trying to make yourself feel good. And where we each draw the circle around what is considered within the category of constructive manipulation will depend on how much healing we do from our past. We may justify certain actions as harmless at one time in our life, but as we become more self-responsible and able to deal with consequences head on, we may see more options for greater honesty and clarity in our relationship with our daughters.

Manipulation crosses the line from constructive to destructive when such actions aim to hurt another, actually harm another (our own self included), and are *conscious*. By the way, *unconscious* manipulative tendencies can also be destructive when old wounds keep us feeling like victims when we truly aren't. We'll focus very little on destructive manipulation because I seriously doubt you would have picked up this book if you were someone who consciously sets out to harm or control others for purely self-serving reasons. Nevertheless, we're all capable of less than desirable behavior, especially if we fear for our survival, even when no actual threats exist. Below are a few examples as may relate to you and your daughter:

- You tell her a lie because you don't want to face the consequences of your own behavior. For instance, she asks you if you saw who hit her car while it was parked. You're the one who dented it, but you lie and say you have no idea.
- You withdraw a portion of her college fund to pay for debt you incurred unrelated to her. But you tell her the money invested for her has decreased because the stock market tanked, and you've never given her access to her account login.
- You fabricate a story about a best friend having cancer so that you can enlist her sympathy because you know she has a soft spot for the emotional pain someone suffers at the potential

loss of a loved one. In fact, her own best friend had recently died of breast cancer.

I'm sure you can come up with many of your own examples and scenarios. I simply want to convey to you that often we have more choices than we think we have and rarely do we have to resort to manipulation. The key is we will not always get what we want, but generally if we're self-reliant and have good support systems we can get our needs met with direct communication. Hence, our reliance on manipulation significantly decreases as we truly distinguish between our wants versus our needs, and we allow people the right to say no to us.

So, whether you like to believe it or not, you have probably resorted to various types of manipulation in your life and with your daughter. And it's possible that such actions have influenced how she has perceived you throughout her life. Owning and fessing up to this possibility may just be one of the many openings to come in developing a healthier relationship with yourself and with her.

Sugar and Spice Exercise: Have I Been Manipulative?

Please take some time at your convenience to assess ways in which you felt manipulated by your own mother. Next, ask yourself if any of what you discover has affected how you parented your own daughter and if you, too, have engaged in any forms of manipulation, either constructive or potentially destructive. Then, try to assess the underlying fears that may have driven your actions. For instance, were you afraid of disapproval, disconnection, or criticism? Most importantly, shame or blame?

When you're ready, let's move on to identifying your "too nice" quotient.

CHAPTER 4

What Is Your "Too Nice" Quotient—TNQ

Thus far, I've used the phrase "too nice" but haven't really defined what I mean by this and why I use the quotation marks. First, let's look at the actual definitions and usages of the noun nice. You might be surprised. According to Merriam-Webster (online dictionary: https://www.merriam-webster.com/dictionary/nice), nice has many definitions. To name a few:

1. "Polite, kind.
2. Pleasing, agreeable. b. Appropriate, fitting. c. Well executed.
3. Socially acceptable. b. Virtuous, respectable.
4. Precision and delicacy.
5. Showing fastidious or finicky tastes, particular. b. Exacting in requirements or standards."

These are all pretty standard and familiar uses of the word. But I wonder if you've ever heard of the following definition. This is the one I've heard many years ago that really stood out to me, coming from the history and etiology of *nescience* (https://www.

merriam-webster.com/dictionary/nescience#etymology). Accordingly, *nice* comes from the late Latin *nescientia*, from Latin *nescient-, nesciens*, present participle of *nescire* not to know, from *ne-* not + *scire* to know. In other words, *nice* can also translate to "pretending not to know".

Why is this relevant? Well, often when we're telling our daughters, or we've been told ourselves, to be "nice" we're actually saying or hearing, "Don't acknowledge what you know to be true"—i.e., to deny reality. While it's okay sometimes to turn the other cheek when it makes the most sense in a moment, having a guiding principle to ignore our truth or to not deal with things head-on can certainly be a problem.

Here's a fun example of a moment with my daughter, Tiffany, who was probably about four years old at the time of this incident. We were at the grocery store waiting to check out and she points to the gentleman ahead of us in line and, without any malice whatsoever, she enthusiastically reports, "Mommy, that's the biggest nose I've ever seen!" I froze for a moment, with a myriad of emotions and responses churning in my brain like a body of muddy water just after a torrential downpour. I had no idea what to say, let alone how to manage that moment. But fortunately, I didn't have to do a thing. This extremely kind and seemingly confident man, who undoubtedly embodied a nose much larger than the average bear, very softly leaned over and said, "Why, yes, it is—would you like to touch it?"

Tiffany, with much delight and excitement despite her often-shy demeanor to strangers, reached out and gave his nose a gentle once over, appearing quite satisfied with the outcome of this scenario. I then thanked the gentleman for his grace with the situation. He smiled, gave a quick wink to my daughter and me, and off we went about our day.

Having grown up as first generation American with both parents having come to this country as persecuted immigrants without the most polished English-speaking skills, they most definitely wanted to assimilate into the culture and to raise their children to fit the cultural norms. Being taught to "be nice" was high on the list lest you wish to be considered mean. Unfortunately, only having these two options at play significantly limited the possible responses to the variety of life circumstances. I certainly didn't want to be a "mean" girl so when I heard the common phrase from my folks, "Shhhh, don't say that, it's mean," or "Just be nice," I took it to heart.

Funnily though, my parents weren't all that "nice" to one another, to us kids, or about others in the world when behind closed doors. They called each other names, threw things at one another, and often said quite derogatory things about other people. So needless to say, I had a lot of negative dialogue swirling around in my head and I was ashamed of many of my impulsive thoughts. While I certainly wasn't perfect at keeping all that negative noise at bay, fortunately once an adult and parent I became better at discerning what my true feelings were versus the negative diatribe of noises stemming from my parents.

Based on this little background detour, I'm sure you can imagine the many impulses I would have had to handle the situation with my daughter and with the man we'll call nose man. Fortunately, by that time in my life, I'd become conscious of the whole "too nice" protocol and had already consciously set my mind and my parenting style to allow my daughter alternate responses outside of the two categories of mean/rude versus nice. Especially if her motives seemed pure and innocent. In the case of nose man, my daughter was purely expressing her observation as she might comment on a beautiful sycamore tree in the forest being the biggest she'd ever seen. She wasn't being rude at all. And nose man, at least on the surface, had made peace with the size of his snout and didn't carry any shame about it. This allowed him to be open to the curious exchange with Tiffany.

After that interaction at the grocery store, I tried to reflect on what I would have done had nose man been less gracious or carried insecurity about his nose. I probably would have said something to try to be soothing but also simultaneously not wanting my daughter to feel shame or guilt as if she had done anything wrong. Let's say he would have remarked angrily and told me to better control my daughter and the things she says to others. I might have replied, "So sorry, sir, that your feelings were hurt by what she said. I'm certain my daughter intended no harm and was only sharing her curious observation." Or something to that effect. And then I would have likely explained to Tiffany, at the earliest possible moment, that she'd said nothing wrong but that sometimes people's feelings are easily hurt so we need to be cautious about what we say to them or how we say it. I don't really know precisely what I would have blurted out, but it would have been from the perspective of using the circumstance as one of the many learning moments in life.

I share this story in such detail because I imagine you have had many of your own moments where you were shamed or censored by a caregiver or other person who may have been instrumental in creating an underlying, maybe over-the-top niceness. On some level, like me, you may have grown to resent this type of boxing in but didn't have a voice for it. So, it's possible that while you wanted to be nice so as to avoid the alternatives, you inadvertently created some challenges or even contradictions in your parenting style and you may be paying that price with your now not-so-nice daughter.

TAKE THE TEST: Just How "Too-Nice" Are You?

After treating hundreds of "too-nice" moms (in the sense of the pretending not to know types), I've developed the following questionnaire to help identify the major indicators. By providing a detailed overview and familiar points of reference, the results of this test can serve as a valuable tool in helping discover if you have fallen into the "too-nice" trap.

Don't be surprised if you identify with many, or even most of these questions. The "too-nice" mom syndrome happens in every state, region, and family group and shows no favoritism to intelligence, creativity, gender, race, or social class. Read the following twenty-five statements and choose the response that best describes how you feel most of the time, then add up your total score.

Please note this is not meant to be an accurate predictor or explanation of how your relationship with your daughter went awry or was never really on track to begin with. No doubt you raised your daughter with the best of intentions and the best skill set you were given and then further developed on your own. I want this to be an exploratory process to possibly create some new ways of conceptualizing your relationship with your daughter. So please don't spend too much time belaboring your responses. There are no wrong or right answers! Also, I'd like you to answer these questions from three points of view with regards to how you felt 1) as a child, 2) as an adult woman, and 3) specifically with reference to your relationship with your grown daughter.

Never (0 points)
Seldom (1 point)
Sometimes (2 points)
Pretty often (3 points)
Most of, if not all, the time (4 points)

Give yourself a 0, 1, 2, 3, or 4 according to your answer to each statement.

Child / Adult Woman / With Daughter
(C) (AW) (WD)

___ ___ ___ 1. I feel unloved.

___ ___ ___ 2. I feel disrespected.

___ ___ ___ 3. I refrain from saying what I think for fear of hurting my daughter's feelings.

___ ___ ___ 4. I feel powerless or out of control.

___ ___ ___ 5. I make up or embellish stories or make excuses because I'm afraid to tell the truth.

___ ___ ___ 6. I resort to people-pleasing rather than thinking of my own needs first.

___ ___ ___ 7. I easily alter my opinions about things or situations with others to fit in or be liked.

___ ___ ___ 8. I try to fix things for others.

___ ___ ___ 9. I don't let my daughter take responsibility for their (her) actions or I am quick to step in to smooth things over.

___ ___ ___ 10. I'm afraid of conflict.

___ ___ ___ 11. I go out of my way to be nice to people (my daughter) even when I'm angry with them (her) or when they (she) have (has) been unkind or abusive to me.

___ ___ ___ 12. I put myself down so others (she) won't feel bad or just because I don't really like myself.

___ ___ ___ 13. I compromise my own needs, so others (my daughter) won't feel bad.

___ ___ ___ 14. I overcompensate with kind gestures or offer favors for others (my daughter) for mistakes I might have made.

___ ___ ___ 15. I get my feelings easily hurt.

___ ___ ___ 16. I go out of my way to do kind deeds to win the approval of others (my daughter).

___ ___ ___ 17. I feel others are (my daughter is) ungrateful for all that I have done for them (her).

___ ___ ___ 18. I find I expect a little, or even a lot, of special treatment because of all I do/have done for others (my daughter).

___ ___ ___ 19. I engage in unhealthy behaviors because I feel stressed out by things/people/responsibilities (my daughter), e.g., overeat/undereat, drink alcohol, or use other substances, gamble or shop too much, etc.

___ ___ ___ 20. I have difficulty saying no, or I say yes when I mean no.

___ ___ ___ 21. I worry about others (my daughter) too much.

___ ___ ___ 22. I experience anxiety (i.e., fear when there is no real danger occurring).

___ ___ ___ 23. I get disappointed in myself or others (my daughter).

___ ___ ___ 24. I have high expectations of myself and others (my daughter).

___ ___ ___ 25. I feel others have (my daughter has) too high of expectations of me and/or that I am a disappointment to others (her).

___ ___ ___ YOUR TOTAL SCORE FOR EACH COLUMN

Once you've finished and added up your score from each perspective, refer to the evaluation below to discover where you land on the "too-nice" spectrum.

Note: If you scored between 0 and 5 in the third column, then I'd be a little surprised if you picked up this book for any reason other than sheer curiosity. It's possible that you don't identify yourself as having any of the characteristics expressed in the statements above, or maybe I failed to state them in ways that would resonate with you. If so, then for that I am sorry. Or you are reading this more to understand the perspective of your daughter, but you don't really believe you have any part in how that all occurred. Maybe your daughter was raised by someone other than you and now you want to have a relationship with her even though you have little to do with her life other than creating her. However, if you do feel that your relationship with your daughter and her current state of being is in part because of your actions, then you could be in denial regarding a few areas. In any case, you got here somehow, so hopefully some of the descriptions below will strike a responsive chord, regardless of your actual score.

For simplicity's sake, I've subdivided the scoring into four levels. Please note the descriptions are on a continuum. Your score could reflect a level one while the description you read matches a level three.

Level One:	6–24 points
Level Two:	25–49 points
Level Three:	50–74 points
Level Four:	75–100 points

With Regards to How You Felt as a Child

Level One: You probably suffered low amounts of pain from emotional distress. You may not have experienced your childhood as wounding, you may have done some healing work through therapy with your family of origin, or you may have had some amazing resources or people in your life who allowed you to experience the difficulties that were present in your life in a much less debilitating way. Or you may simply be gifted with a super-resilient constitution wherein even the worst of events have rolled off your back, leaving you relatively unscathed. However, you may have a few items you scored with a two or higher and these specific areas may warrant some noting. In any case, it never hurts to go the extra mile and clear out whatever residual emotional wounds still exist.

Level Two: You likely experienced some significant distress in your day-to-day living during your childhood and in your relationships. While you were probably not a complete prisoner of suffering, you might have, at times, been driven by fear and anger rather than by conscious, rational decision-making. You may have had disruptions in your relationships with others outside of family such as with friends, peers, or teachers.

No doubt your world did not feel entirely safe, and you may have become prone to defensiveness due to easily hurt feelings. You may have even taught yourself to cut off from relationships before they became too intense so that you wouldn't get hurt. But you fared okay and weren't completely devastated or unable to develop a voice of your own, at least somewhat, and possibly even great functionality.

Level Three: You probably experienced a great deal of emotional pain and suffering, possibly having been sexually molested, threatened by abandonment, or physically and/or psychologically abused. You did not learn that you deserved to be loved and respected, let alone honored and allowed to have preferences and differences of opinions from others.

You may have believed you didn't deserve anything better and may have experienced helplessness and hopelessness at times throughout your youth. You may have rationalized traumatizing behavior from others as something you caused or deserved. Equally disturbing, you may have failed to even recognize that these wounding behaviors were wrong. On top of that, you may not even have recognized or taken seriously the possibility that *you* might have had to participate in wounding others, rationalizing that you had no other choice.

Level Four: You were required to sacrifice your needs for the sake of others, or it's what you perceived to be your only chance for survival. You lived in a psychological prison with maximum security, not able to see any escape. Because of intense shame, self-doubt, or self-hatred, you may not have been able to accept acts of kindness even when right in front of you. You probably became so accustomed to being mistreated that you may not have known that any other kind of treatment existed. My guess is that you desperately wanted to feel better, but you had no one to turn to for help or you may not have trusted anyone who tried to offer any help.

At this moment, just note where you landed from the child's perspective and then continue understanding from your current perspective as an adult woman, and then in relation to your experience of yourself as a mother with your adult daughter.

Score as an Adult Woman

I believe many of us would have liked to see our adulthood as a separate entity from our childhoods; especially those of us who felt mistreated, experienced trauma, or generally had a tough time in our youth, for whatever reasons. But, in my experience, our perspective of ourselves from childhood does inform our view of ourselves in adulthood, at least to some degree; especially if we haven't undergone conscious healing to connect the dots. I could be wrong, but let's see if your score matches up with this premise.

Level One: Overall you probably feel pretty good about yourself and in relation to others. You may hit a few bumps on the road of life, but you likely have gathered enough tools and equipment along the way to face most challenges and responsibilities, except for maybe a tsunami. And if you got to this point having had a much higher score from the child perspective, extra kudos to you. You've probably done some remarkable self-work to get to this place of inner peace and well-being. Nevertheless, I encourage you to pay attention to the specific items on which you identified with a two or higher as these may reflect some remnants of the past worthy of some further housecleaning.

Level Two: With this range, you may feel like things go pretty well most of the time, but you could find yourself particularly sensitive in certain areas, kind of like spiking a high fever for a day or so and then needing some extra tender-loving care to get back to your overall sense of well-being. Or maybe you experience a low-grade sensitivity more often than not, like having a low-grade fever, where you can still function and feel joy but just not at the level you desire.

Level Three: Again, these levels are just meant to guide your awareness of how much residual trauma you may still be carrying from your childhood and/or from difficult life situations in your adult world. Within this range, you may have, to some degree, recreated some of the pain from your past in your adult relationships. In other words, you may have unconsciously become a magnet for mistreatment from others, having not learned how to set healthy boundaries. You may not know how to provide self-love and nurturance, let alone feel deserving of it. Or, if your score from the perspective of how you perceived yourself as a child is significantly lower than your score as an adult woman, you may have seriously been dealt a bad poker hand (e.g., suffered multiple losses, had a bad car accident leaving irreparable body damage, having darkened your perspective on the world from a once rosier scene). In either case there's no need for doom or gloom here. All can be healed. So, again, just notice which of the items you scored the highest numbers with. Recognize that prior emotional wounds or traumas may have had a greater impact on your parenting style, and ultimately, how these may have affected your relationship with your daughter along the way.

Level four: You're probably plagued by chronic shame. (Note: Shame will be fully discussed in Chapter Seven.) You may continually wonder why you feel unhappy and chronically hurt in your relationships. You may feel like a victim of bad circumstances or constantly blame yourself for things and take on more responsibility for others than is actually your fair share. You may experience yourself as utterly powerless and have difficulty seeing available choices and options. You may have become a walking magnet for mistreatment. Abusive people have radar for spotting you because they are consciously or unconsciously searching for someone to exploit, and you display all the hallmarks of the perfect target. You may have desired to have children of your own so you could make right all the wrongs that were done to you.

With all this, you may also be in an emotionally wounding or abusive relationship right now, e.g., with a significant other, a parent, or even with your own daughter. If so, especially if the abuse is severe, like physical battering, you may need more immediate help addressing these issues to get yourself out of immediate danger. This book alone will not be enough. You, too, can become a healthy-hearted, happy woman, but you may need to direct your energy first and foremost toward yourself and let your daughter know you love her dearly but need to focus on your own healing first.

How You Feel in Your Relationship with Your Adult Daughter

Level One: Your struggle is real, no doubt. And I'm glad you're reading this book because you will likely be able to prevent things from deteriorating further. You may even discover that with a few tweaks in your own perception of the realities of a healthy mother—adult daughter relationship, things might feel and get better quite quickly. In other words, maybe your adult daughter isn't really all that sassy and rude but just asserting herself and her independence in a way that is foreign to you. Or maybe you said or did something to her that she feels hurt by and hasn't been able to tell you, so now she's holding a grudge. Once you heal the wound, you can move forward. If so, you just need a new treasure map so as not to get sidetracked by irrelevant detours. And if you scored higher on either or both of the other measures—way to go for having done some valuable healing within yourself to have avoided what could have been more of a train wreck.

Level Two: In this range, you probably experience quite a few rough spots in your relationship with your adult daughter. You're not close like you once had been, and you scratch your head at times wondering what the heck went wrong. That question from Chapter Two—"Is It Me or Is It She?"—may come up a bunch. Fear not! You've got this one way or another. If you scored in this range or higher on the other two indices, very likely if you clean your own historical wounds or those you carry from other sources and share your discoveries with your gal, I'm confident her 'tude will change. And if it doesn't, then you can pretty much answer your question and leave the ball in her court if she wants to do her part to heal with you or not.

Level Three: This speaks to a pretty dire situation. It's probably a combo pack of stuff you've brought to the table and things you may not know about your daughter's life. You may have inadvertently re-created your own childhood wounds (maybe taking a different shape) with her and neither of you know how to speak to this. She may have gone into her own therapy and was led to focus on all the ills of her childhood only to discover that she had issues with you she never knew how to speak about. Hence, she may be asserting her own right to heal and not know how to include you. The explanations can go on and on. I certainly don't know the details or what's going on in her mind. But I can say that I trust that if you sincerely practice the principles and exercises outlined in the coming chapters, you will open the door for greater communication and understanding of the underlying issues needing to be addressed. If not, then all the more reason to adopt the fundamental essence of this book, i.e., you are only responsible for that which you can control. Once your daughter reaches adulthood and independence, there is no more that you can control.

Level Four: Things must certainly feel as if in crisis mode at this level. There's definitely more than meets the eye here. Maybe some mental health issues are coming out either within yourself or within her or a resurgence of those that were present in the past. She may be keeping some big, deep, dark secret from you and is pushing you away, not knowing how to do anything differently. I wish I could give you a better explanation, but I can't without knowing your particular history and situation with your daughter. And even if you could give me your full perspective, without your daughter's I still would have no definitive answers. Hence, I would still simply be speculating. What I can say, however, is that my heart feels for your pain—but there are reasons to keep moving forward toward mending what's broken. I, too, have had several moments of my own despair along this journey and so too have countless other mothers. Also, regardless of what you do on your end, you may have to take a step back and accept that if your daughter chooses to push you away you can know in your heart of hearts that you tried everything that you could do!

Suggestions on Tying the Three Perspectives Together

Because there are four levels for each of the three different columns, there would be far too many possible permutations to address. We can make comparisons and observations of differences by looking at each column in relation to each other column, e.g., 1 with 2, 2 with 3, 1 with 3, and 1, 2, and 3 all together. And the number of options increases exponentially. You could be a level one from C, a level two from AW, and a level 3 with your daughter. Its combinations and permutations are far too many to address each combo separately. Of course, feel free to do your own analysis if you're so inclined. But for our purposes here, I just want you to have the opportunity to take a moment to notice if, or where, there are differences. For instance, maybe there is a trend. If so, what is your trend? What stands out to you about where the most focus of repair needs to land?

In general, and I can't prove this, but in my experience if we carried childhood wounds into our adult lives, they're likely to continue to wreak havoc somewhere; if not everywhere. So, it's important to pay attention to whatever residual carryover you discover. Also, it is possible that your level regarding your perspective of yourself was low, but you still have a high range with your daughter. If so, there may be something about her specifically that triggers old wounds. Again, just try to stay open-minded and non-judgmental about both you and your daughter.

Now that you've done this exercise, hopefully you have a more conscious appreciation for where your pain and suffering lies. Regardless of the levels you found, hopefully you will find some new concepts throughout the remaining chapters to improve the quality of the relationship you have with yourself, and ultimately with your adult daughter.

Now let's have some fun and find out what type of role you play in the "too-nice" mom's club.

CHAPTER 5

"Too Nice" Mom's Club

There's a movie called the First Wife's Club, made in 1996. In case you're unfamiliar with it, it essentially depicts several divorcees seeking revenge on their exes for having sought out younger women. Clearly not the same as this club, but it did inspire the title of this chapter, "The Too Nice Mom's Club", aka the TNMC. Who can belong? You, of course! Don't worry, there are no membership fees or requirements for admission, simply that you identify as being a "too nice" mom. By the way, even if you're not perceived by your daughter as all that nice in her eyes, that doesn't mean your intentions are anything but good and meant to be loving and supportive so you can ultimately be closer to your adult daughter.

For starters, "too nice" moms come in all different sizes and shapes with a myriad of characteristics. In other words, there's no one-size-fits all "too-nice" mom type. While there are certainly overlapping characteristics among those in the club, some unique differences stand out. So just like when you read your horoscope based on your astrological sign and then you read the descriptions of the other signs, you'll probably find that you can resonate or overlap with several features of the other signs. You may find that only a select few truly identify your sub-type.

By the way, you may look at the sub-types below and how I've named them and cringe, as they may sound harsh. However, these are not meant to be insulting. Rather, I'm asking you to try to have a sense of humor about yourself and fess up to some of the qualities or underlying driving forces that may have rubbed your daughter the wrong way, despite all your benevolent intentions. It is through a more light-hearted lens, as opposed to through a shaming lens, that we can gain insight and grow. After all, I hope you have already received my underlying message: **I know you've done your best and am sure you have been an amazing mom in so many ways!** But in the end, your receiver hasn't necessarily registered the messages you've been sending. So, it's good to look at yourself from a more objective view with the possibility that some of your intent was misperceived or backfired all together. Again, any wounds we carried over from our own childhood and/or adult experiences outside of motherhood may have bled into our mothering style, resulting in protective gear of various characteristics.

So, now let's meet the moms of the TNMC!

Nervous Nelly

Nelly, a fifty-two-year-old teacher who raised two girls and a boy, was born to a highly overprotective mom. Both her parents were first generation immigrants who had been persecuted in their countries of origin. Both suffered tremendous psychological and physical trauma and embodied a lot of fear. Nelly was not spared awareness of the hardships they had endured. And as is common to many children raised by immigrants who fled danger, Nelly adopted and absorbed many of her parents' fears by osmosis.

Of course, Nelly's parents wanted nothing more than for their children (one daughter and one son) to have an easier life than they'd had, and they did their best to put their traumatic memories to rest. Yet, nevertheless, their scars inadvertently ended up transmitting to their children. Nelly, who took more risks than her brother, suffered perpetual worry and anxiety. She tried hard to camouflage this for her own children but both her son, the youngest, and her older daughter, being highly empathetic, sensed anxiety like a mama bear knowing hunters are near her cubs.

Nelly would say things to her kids like, "There's nothing to worry about, everything will be all right." But they could see in her face and her eyes that she was quivering and thinking, "Oh my, what will I do if this occurs, or if that occurs, or even worse if this occurs." She had a never-ending list of the "what ifs."

Sometimes her daughter, Maegan, could hear her mom crying at night to her friends or to Maegan's father about all the things that she was worried about. Nelly's son, who identified more with his dad and took more cues from him, moved through his youth a bit more unscathed, whereas Maegan took the brunt. Eventually, when Maegan left the nest and started living on her own, she began taking extreme risks just to prove to herself there was nothing to fear in life. At times she behaved recklessly and impulsively, as if to teach her mother that she was wrong about the world. This created a cataclysmic divide between her and her mother.

Nelly came to see me after Maegan, then twenty-eight-years-old, lost it on her and told her she was overbearing and to just leave her alone once and for all. Mind you, this wasn't the first time her daughter had complained about her mom's overprotective nature, but this time she was much fiercer and really meant that she was going to shut her mom out of her life permanently. Nelly was beside herself and couldn't imagine not being part of the next chapters of Maegan's life.

Their work was about coming to a middle ground so that Maegan could live her life free and clear of unnecessary, torturous worry, but also find a balance of responsibility and self-care. Nelly's job was to find some new adventures and take new risks long ago stifled. Then they could have some common ground to share their discoveries and put an end to their polarization.

Characteristics of Nervous Moms

Nervous moms can have many positive qualities such as:

- Ability to mitigate danger.
- Always have a back-up plan.
- Can present a realistic counter side to the perpetual optimist who isn't at all grounded in reality.

But this subtype can also come along with qualities that can be overbearing at times, particularly if the anxiety permeates all aspects of their lives. Some of these qualities include:

- Can be controlling.
- Have difficulty resting in the quiet moments.
- Appear tense and wound up.
- Jumps to conclusions.
- Can become a nay-sayer.

Next, we'll meet Woo Woo Wilma.

Woo Woo Wilma

Wilma, a fifty-something year old Pilates instructor and mother of three (two sons and a daughter) came to see me with her daughter, Veronica, aged thirty-two. Wilma was raised in a family with three other siblings, and one might say all in all her life was pretty good. However, from her eyes, she felt she was pressured to carry out the life of her mother's unrealized dreams; that is, for Wilma to go to college and enjoy a flourishing career in a stable, high-paying industry.

Wilma's mom could never afford to go to college and felt trapped in a dead-end job. On top of that, her mom was a stickler for details and precision. She ran a tight ship at home and did not stand for anything outside the realm of "normalcy." Wilma, on the other hand, danced to a different tune. She was highly creative, and her dreams and passions fell outside the box, so to speak. As an example, she envisioned creating communities and villages with fairtrade organic foods and products with collective parenting so everyone would be healthy, and no one would ever feel alone. Her free-spirited nature, however, was highly pooh-poohed in her family and she was continually encouraged to walk the straight line. "You have to get a real job with a paycheck, like a banker or nurse," they would say. Without conscious awareness, Wilma became increasingly drawn toward what some might call the woo woo world, loving tarot cards and astrology, studying ancient herbal remedies, attending spiritual awakening circles, and a number of other less mainstream practices. At times her mother thought she was out of her mind and would put strong restrictions on Wilma's exploration of alternative life practices.

Once Wilma entered adulthood, she made her way to community college (trying to please her mother) while living on financial aid. She grappled with different jobs and found her way to health and fitness with Pilates singing to her because of some sports injuries during high school. But she was not fulfilled.

As time went on, she also became increasingly drawn toward her earlier passions and had great fun hosting small gatherings with her friends for tea and tarot readings. She eventually married and had children of her own, vowing to give them creative license to explore anything and everything.

As a mom, Wilma took her role very seriously and, of course, wanted to provide a stable and creative environment for her children to thrive. Veronica, her only daughter, was definitely going to get the freedom to explore her own passions, which for Wilma had been suppressed during her childhood.

While growing up, Wilma's woo woo interests intrigued Veronica. Up until about age thirteen, Veronica would always invite her friends over to her house because her mom would do psychic readings and perform seances, etc., sometimes to the dismay of other parents. But because Wilma was also known in her community for being good-hearted, she was tolerated for her out-of-the-box shenanigans.

As Veronica entered her teens, her desire to get more serious about school and assert more of her extraordinarily practical side began to come out. Turns out, Veronica was far more similar to her maternal grandmother. She liked things orderly, and she was drawn more toward realism, especially when it came down to thinking about her future. She set out to achieve a bachelor's degree, and possibly go even further in her education by attending graduate school. While her mom certainly supported her academic ventures, there were many moments where it was clear that Wilma felt a bit betrayed by her daughters "disloyalty."

Eventually, around Veronica's third year of college, she started distancing herself from her mother and felt kind of embarrassed that her mother was so different from her other friends' moms. What she once adored about her mother was no longer as cool as she once thought, and her focus became much more about settling into her own concept of responsibility and independence.

To say the least, Wilma was incredibly hurt and sought my help. And it certainly took a while for them to come to terms with their differences. Gratefully, they eventually found a way to respect one another and realize that they could each enjoy their own paths to happiness while simultaneously enjoying their overlapping love for one another. Wilma learned to step back when Veronica was in intense study mode and Veronica occasionally invited her friends over to the house for psychic readings and to sample some of her mother's delicious chocolate creations.

Characteristics of Woo Woo Moms

Woo woo moms exude numerous endearing and delightful qualities. These moms are often:

- Spontaneous and free-spirited—going where the wind blows them.
- Great story tellers.
- Able to see past the five senses and three dimensions.
- Mystical and enchanting, especially to outsiders who feel stuck in their lives.
- Highly intuitive.

The potential downside to these types of moms is that they can frustrate those who desire more of a boots-on-the-ground approach to life, structure, discipline, and direction. This is especially the case when dealing with another who has very prescribed goals and desired achievements in the mainstream and/or someone who gets anxious without structure.

Perfect Pia

Pia, a stay-at-home mom in her late fifties, operated to the tune of "things must be as perfect as they can be." If things fell short of desired alignment, she would go to the ends of the Earth to find a way to make things right. Her mother would say she was born this way, but her family of origin also certainly supported and reinforced this as one of her finest qualities. Pia naturally assumed since this worked well for her, she would generate a similar family environment when she embarked on raising children with her wife, Kelli. On the other hand, Kelli was much more lackadaisical and wanted to create a more serene environment. She tolerated Pia's perfectionism but tried her best not to engage. However, since Pia was the primary caregiver to their daughter, Astrid, her perfectionistic influence prevailed.

For Pia, nothing became more important than being the perfect mom. In her mind, that meant catering to Astrid's every whim so that Astrid would never want for anything. Unbeknownst to Pia, she was compensating for her own lack of self-worth and did not realize that she was inadvertently creating in Astrid a sense that she could never meet up to her mother's standards. Pia was so hard on herself when things didn't go well or look good to the outside world, that even though all she wanted was for her daughter to grow up feeling like the world was her oyster, Astrid feared she would be a disappointment to her mom. And, at some point, she just stopped trying. In her teens, she kept her grades up and pretended everything was okay, but deep inside she began struggling with depression. She stopped confiding in her mom about her troubles and woes, got into some drugs, and started skipping school. Because she was a good student who knew how to play the system, she avoided getting into trouble.

Astrid hid her depression. She grew increasingly resentful toward Pia and even toward her other mom. She believed Kelli should have intervened in Pia's obsession about things being perfect and spared Astrid from feeling as if she had to emulate her mother to be accepted. During her early to mid-twenties, Pia became irritated with Astrid, to the point of demanding that Astrid explain why she had become so distant. Astrid avoided her mother's pleas for several years until she had children of her own and her mother began constantly criticizing her parenting. Pia, of course, didn't think she was being critical. She thought she was being helpful and informative, passing along her acquired wisdom as a parent, now grandmother.

Finally, Astrid couldn't take it anymore, and her sassy and rude came out in full swing. She blurted out, "Mother, no one is ever going to be as perfect as you. And quite frankly, you're far from perfect yourself. Go get a life."

Pia was devastated. She had no idea of the impact her need for perfection had on her daughter, who she loved so deeply. She had no idea how her message was being received. She needed to undergo a deep exploration of her own buried childhood wounds and her lack of self-confidence camouflaged by trying to make things just so. She needed to learn to accept that good enough was not the same as failing, but that it is just that—good enough. Eventually, Pia and Astrid began a healing process and Pia learned to step back with her advice or present it with much more sensitivity to Astrid's wound of having felt inadequate in her mother's eyes.

Characteristics of Perfectionistic Moms:

If this description resonates with you, trust me, you are not alone and you bring great qualities to real-life situations requiring precision and orientation to detail. If I need open heart surgery, I'm not looking for a nonchalant, distracted, laid-back, or clown-like surgeon. Rather, I'd want a highly disciplined, detail-oriented perfectionist on my team because perfectionists can bring highly valuable qualities to the table. They often:

- Catch important details about things that, if they were to fall through the cracks, could be very detrimental.
- Do a job well-done.
- Keep chaos at bay.
- Can persevere even under stress.
- Be instrumental in finalizing plans and being prepared with the details.
- Clean and tidy.
- Can read the needs of others.

Where perfectionists sometimes fall short, however, is when a situation or experience is better served with a more relaxed and go-with-the flow approach. They tend to ruminate about things that really won't matter somewhere down the line. They have a hard time looking at the overall picture. They often create unnecessary stress in the moment which they may regret. Having observed my own perfectionistic tendencies, my daughter once so aptly said to me while I was cooking dinner and what I was preparing wasn't turning out right, "Mom, is this really going to bother you in five minutes, or even five hours from now?" It stopped me dead in my tracks of increased frustration, and I looked at her and thought, "Wow, what a wise little girl!" She was only about twelve.

Now let's meet Deprecating Daisy, a mother heavily weighed down with self-doubt and loathing.

Deprecating Daisy

Deprecating Daisy, eldest of two daughters, grew up plagued by feelings of inadequacy. Despite high academic performance, athleticism, and high emotional IQ, she housed a deep underlying sense of worthlessness. Her sister Laura, five years her junior, on the other hand quite surprisingly managed to grow up with solid self-esteem. It was almost as if they had been raised by different mothers. Whereas Laura was cut a lot of slack having been seen as the less bright one, Daisy was held to a much higher standard and, quite frankly, her mother was very hard on her.

Daisy's mother, Gilda, had her own challenges from her family of origin, but she did not ever undertake a journey of healing. Instead, she had developed a false sense of confidence and kind of adopted the old "spare the rod, spoil the child" attitude. We won't even go into Gilda's trauma-ridden childhood. Suffice it to say that it was a shit show in and of itself. Unfortunately for Daisy, her mother took her own suffering out on Daisy (almost her scapegoat) and actively put her down and minimized her accomplishments. For instance, she would say things like, "Don't act too proud or you'll be seen as unattractive," or "Don't think you're so special, anybody can do those things." Daisy just couldn't win.

Sadly, for Daisy, her mother unconsciously passed along her own wounds to her daughter and felt justified in her negative actions toward her. Daisy, however, once she became a mom of two boys and a girl, embarked on a mission to break the cycle of family dysfunction and make sure her children would escape the chains of guilt and shame she endured and create an environment wherein they would ultimately feel good about themselves. She especially tried to prevent feelings of inadequacy in her daughter, Jill. However, what she didn't realize was that she needed to repair her own sense of self first because without doing so she was practicing "do as I say, not as I do." So, while she was pouring all of her heart into boosting her children's self-confidence, she was openly demonstrating self-deprecation and low self-worth.

Her daughter, Jill, grew up feeling bad for her mom and kept wanting to soothe her and tell her that everything would be okay. At some point, however, she grew tired of having to nurture her mom and feeling like she needed to re-mother her. She saw all of the great qualities in her mom, but she resented being the one to have to keep raising the mirror for her to see a positive reflection. She wanted her mom to "fix" herself.

Jill wanted to embrace the confidence her mother was so desperately trying to bestow upon her, but she just couldn't identify with her mother as a positive role model. In service of her own protection and not wanting to be swallowed up by her mother's insecurities, Jill developed a heightened sense of entitlement and arrogance. Eventually she began taking advantage of her mom, knowing that she could get just about anything she wanted. Her Dad was a bit stricter than her mom, but quite frankly, his daughter was the apple of his eye, and he would cave to Jill's demands as well. Jill's dismissive and rude attitude sky-rocketed during her teens and early twenties, basically demanding that her parents, particularly her mom, continue to fund her lifestyle without regard for her own need to become a self-sufficient adult.

Mind you, Jill wasn't really a narcissist. That is, someone who lacks empathy and disregards the needs of others. However, she certainly developed characteristics that could lead one to believe she was uncaring and self-centered if one were to observe how she treated her mom. On the contrary, she felt deeply for her mother's pain, but she needed to protect herself, creating a defensive reaction. Essentially, she took a 180 degree turn from her mother, exuding oodles of confidence to the point of arrogance.

It took quite a bit of time. Slowly but surely, Daisy healed from the shame deep within her and began displaying greater self-confidence. She pursued a master's degree in psychology and eventually became a licensed practitioner. Jill watched on the sidelines with a lot of sarcastic commentary. But once she dove into psychotherapy and had children of her own, she started seeking out a more loving relationship with her mom, taking to heart that there is more than meets the eye; especially when it comes to understanding one's mother.

Characteristics of Deprecating Moms:

Deprecating moms, like Daisy, can bring great value to a relationship. They can be very endearing and draw in kindness and compassion from otherwise hardened individuals. They often:

- Create a high level of safety and vulnerability in others who also lack self-worth.
- Minimize the experience of shame or guilt in others.
- Encourage deeper self-disclosure in others, particularly with regards to insecurities.
- Bring a tone of acceptance.
- Create humility in others.

While self-deprecation in small doses can have certain upsides, there are also several downsides, especially when constant and extreme. Self-deprecation can inspire pity in others, possibly leading to others needing to repel them. Self-deprecators lose out on self-love and joys that come from trying new things and making mistakes for fear of being judged and having more things to feel bad about oneself. They can make their world smaller than it needs to be in order to not feel exposed and hurt by others. And daughters of self-deprecators can end up feeling like they need to take care of their moms rather than the reverse, leading to resentment and anger—just like it had for Jill. Don't despair if this speaks to you. You must simply work on self-love and healing the shame that suffocates you.

Lastly, let's meet Friendly Frida.

Friendly Frida

Frida, raised by her mother, Joanne, who was a very stoic woman, developed into the type who needed to befriend everyone from the neighbor next door to the one-time Amazon delivery person. According to Frida, her mom believed that working hard was the most important thing in the world, above all else. Why? "Because my parents were reckless and lazy, and I'm not going to recreate that wound in my child." Joanne would also say, "Frida, I will make it my life goal to make sure you will have an easier life than I had and that you'll never have to do without!" (All in reference to financial stability.) But Frida, who admittedly described herself as a high contact person with strong bonding desires, would have traded her mother's riches in finances for more cuddles and quality time. Hence, while Joanne believed she was righting the wrongs from her childhood, she created a different kind of wound in her own daughter in a sense of loneliness and longing for love and affection.

Frida eventually married when she was thirty-four and she and her husband embarked on the baby-making process when she was thirty-six. Sadly, she underwent two miscarriages and years of infertility until she was finally blessed with her dream come true. She had a baby girl named Kayla at age forty-one. Because it had taken so long to conceive, by the time she had Kayla she almost wanted to bypass motherhood and just have a new pal in her life. Nevertheless, she performed all her motherly duties, but the differentiation between mother and daughter became increasingly blurred. Their relationship was so close, it was even to the point of being exclusive. When Frida wasn't at work as a part-time office manager, she focused all her attention on her daughter. They did everything together, becoming inseparable. So much so that she and her husband ended up divorcing when Kayla was eight because he didn't feel he mattered at all.

Naturally, at first Kayla thought this was awesome and she loved the attention that made her feel ever so special. From Frida's point of view, she believed she was showering Kayla with endless love and acceptance, unaware that she wasn't necessarily meeting the developmental needs of her child or for herself. For instance, neither actively participated in their own age-appropriate friendships. There was no encouragement for independence or for differing points of view. It was almost as if the unspoken code was that they had to be one and the same person. And, on top of all that, because Frida wasn't relying on her own friends for support for the adult things going on in her life, she often turned to Kayla to be her confidant. At some point, Kayla even stopped wanting to spend time with her dad because she didn't want to miss out on some new fun adventure she and her mom might have together.

Basically, there was no separation or individuation between Kayla and her mother. (More on the separation/individuation process in Chapter Eleven.) On the rare occasion when Kayla would have a friend or two come over for a sleepover in early adolescence, her mom would assert herself into every part of every conversation and all the games played, and Kayla wanted her there, too. At first her friends were envious of Kayla for having a mom who could be so cool, playful, and fun. But over time, her friends started to think it was kind of weird that Kayla didn't want to disengage from her mom at all and they really didn't want to share with her mom their budding crushes on their peers, their awkwardness about their bodies changing from puberty, etc.

Their dynamic duo held strong until Kayla entered middle school. Not that she didn't still love her mother's undivided attention and being involved in all aspects of her life, but she started to become more and more antsy to experience unique adventures and experiences with her peers, particularly outside of school. However, she felt guilty and worried that she would hurt her mother's feelings. After all, her mother hadn't even started dating following the divorce because she made her whole life about Kayla. She started making up excuses when her mom would create plans for them, saying that she had responsibilities she couldn't get out of. She started to feel more and more trapped, wanting more independence but fearing her mom might have an emotional breakdown.

As Kayla began pulling away from her mom, Frida started enticing her with more and more material things, fantastic weekend getaways, spa treatments, shopping sprees, etc. Because these offerings were quite appealing to Kayla, Frida would often get positive reinforcement by winning back the attention of her daughter. Unconsciously, both of them had entered into a manipulative feedback loop which became increasingly destructive to their relationship. By high school, Kayla had her mom eating out of the palm of her hand and Frida almost became punitive by withholding certain things from Kayla in order to bribe her into spending time with her. The tumult between them became quite fierce at times.

Once Kayla hit adulthood, she was in full-throttle rebellion mode. She hastily moved out and into an apartment with her boyfriend, a living set-up neither she nor her beau could afford. This hurt Frida to the core, with her being completely perplexed as to why her once sugar and spice and everything nice little girl turned into such a bitch! She hadn't realized along the way that what Kayla had really needed from her was for her to be her mother, not necessarily her friend. And now she was being rejected from both roles, not knowing what she had done wrong.

Trapped within a mental hurricane, Frida called me for help, asking me, "How do I get my daughter back?" I said, as compassionately as possible, feeling her pain, "You're asking the wrong question. What you need to be asking is 'How can I build a new and healthy relationship with my adult daughter?'" And we were off and running. Essentially, what Frida and Kayla needed was a total system revamp, and we did just that.

Characteristics of the "Too Friendly" Mom.

Having a mom who wants to be your friend can be so seductive. We look up to our moms when we're growing up and having them want to include us fully in their world can be so validating. They can be so much fun and make you feel as if no one or nothing else matters in the world. Some exceptional qualities of friendly moms can include:

- Being super fun to hang out with.
- Let you slide on tedious responsibilities sometimes because they'd rather you have a good time than sweat the boring stuff.
- Make you feel on top of the world.
- Help you fulfill your dreams and are right there by your side.
- Accelerate your maturity by exposing you to more worldly things.

But just like with the other mothers in the TNMC, there can also be some dire consequences for the overly friendly mom and her relationship with her daughter. For the moms, they can miss out on important aspects of life outside of raising a child, such as friendships with adult friends, enjoying romance, and building career opportunities. This could leave her feeling resentful when her daughter flees the nest and ultimately may have a family of her own. For the daughters, it's just too much pressure. There is a natural power differential between a parent and a child—and this is necessary for development and maturation. And the daughter may develop unrealistic views of relationships and how to create healthy dynamics within them.

Do you identify with any of the descriptions above? Or do you find you have elements of several of them? Keep in mind that many moms can be a mixture of several of these. The idea is to start thinking in terms of your own characteristic style of mothering and how this affects your particular interactions with your daughter.

Sugar and Spice Exercise:

I get it—that was a lot to process! Take a deep breath and congratulate yourself for taking a closer look at the nuances of your mothering style or subtype. Now, make a list of your takeaways, identifying your characteristic mothering style and outlining the pros and cons. What served you well? What didn't? These will be the focus of your attention when you enter the active healing phase of this process. I hope you can see that even with the best of intentions, sometimes our parenting goes awry when informed by unhealed emotional wounds of our own. As such, we can sometimes fall into the trap of having provided the opposite of what we received, hoping to have a better outcome, only to discover that we inevitably created a ground for more wounds. So don't beat yourself up. Instead, try to find a little humor in all of this. And remember, all of this was done out of love. So, even if your daughter is dissing you now or has been for some time, coming back to the core of love will carry you through.

Now let's see what your daughter's Sassy Factor is and how big of a beast you're dealing with.

CHAPTER 6

What's Your Daughter's Sassy Factor?

Okay, so we've identified your "too nice" quotient and covered the subtypes of the TNMC. Now it's time for you to assess your daughter's actual sassy factor. You might discover that it's more severe than you thought, less dire than you believed, or about the same. Again, the choice of the items included wasn't based on any scientifically validated research. Nevertheless, I think you'll find that by addressing the statements below you will get a better sense of where your adult daughter lies on the sassy and rude continuum from your point of view. Mind you, she may have a completely different point of view from yours.

Please read the following twenty-five statements and choose the response that best describes how you feel most of the time. Then add up your total score. There are no wrong or right answers.

Never (0 points)
Seldom (1 point)
Sometimes (2 points)
Pretty often (3 points)
Most of, if not all, the time (4 points)

Give yourself a 0, 1, 2, 3, or 4 according to your answer to each question.

1. She ignores my texts or calls. _____
2. She outspokenly tells me she doesn't want my input on her life. _____
3. She indirectly gives me signs that she doesn't want my input on her life (she dismisses what I say, or cuts conversations short when I'm giving her my opinion, etc.). _____
4. She displays disrespectful gestures (rolls her eyes at me, interrupts me while I'm in mid-sentence and not out of joy and enthusiasm, she uses my credit card without permission, etc.). _____
5. She asks for special favors that require me to give up my own needs. _____
6. She complains about my behavior. _____
7. She becomes easily irritated or annoyed during our interactions. _____
8. She cancels plans with me. (This could be a simple as setting time for a video chat and she bails.) _____
9. She avoids making plans with me (She's too busy at work, she has too much on her mind, her friend's going through a breakup and needs all her spare time, etc.). _____
10. She talks about how I've failed her or have done nothing right. _____
11. She makes sarcastic comments to/about me (beyond her typical baseline). _____
12. She reminds me how much better she feels around people other than me. _____
13. She displays excessive entitlement. _____
14. She fails to display gratitude when I go out of my way to help her with something. _____

15. She contacts me when in crisis but not otherwise. _____
16. She expects me to drop whatever I'm doing to help her out with whatever is going on with her. _____
17. She ridicules my personality, style of dress/hair/makeup, and/or... _____
18. She fails to display empathy toward me. _____
19. She bullies me when I don't succumb to her requests. _____
20. She manipulates/takes advantage of my kindness. _____
21. She threatens to kick me out of her life if I don't (fill in the blank) (e.g., she threatens not to come home for the holidays if you don't do...). _____
22. She lies to or steals from me. _____
23. She's unapologetic when she's been rude to me. _____
24. She shouts at me even when I think we're having a civil conversation. _____
25. She starts arguments with me for no apparent reason. _____

Now add up your score

Level One:	6–24 points
Level Two:	25–49 points
Level Three:	50–74 points
Level Four:	75–100 points

More than likely given that you're reading this book, your score reflects that you perceive your daughter's sassy and rude quotient to be at least at a Level One. If not, you may want to revisit the statements just to make sure you weren't glossing over anything. Or you may want to ask a trusted confidant who has borne witness to your interactions with your daughter. Also, it's quite possible my choice of behaviors indicative of what I believe many people would categorize as "rude" may not resonate with you. Hence, I may have missed something fundamental in your relationship with her and for that I apologize. If I did not capture the examples of what you feel is rude, feel free to make your own list. Plus, some daughters have very strong abilities to camouflage their sense of discord with their mothers, and these mothers just know that something is off and doesn't feel right. This might be your situation. Nevertheless, please read on as you may find some useful tidbits in the descriptions below.

Level One: This is relatively good news. While you may be harboring hurt feelings about whatever rift has interfered with your emotional coziness with your daughter, you're probably just a few steps away from being on the mend and getting to the place you'd like to be with her. Or your daughter may have always been very compliant and this may be the first sign that she's finally ready to individuate from you but just hasn't known how to communicate in a healthy and direct way with you. Please go back and note whether your scoring was consistent in the "seldom" or "sometimes" category, or if you had mostly 0's and 1's and then a few larger numbers throughout. If the latter, then you may want to focus your attention on these areas.

Level Two: We have a little more sass going on here. Not doomsday though, you just might need a bit more healing. More than likely your daughter has become annoyed with you in some way and is feeling entitled to snub you. I'd bet she's hurting inside and wished the two of you were closer and more in sync, but she doesn't have the resources to tell you.

Level Three: No doubt, you're experiencing a fair amount of conflict and can't seem to find a way to be at peace with one another or even be able to spend much quality time together. At times you may want to even write her off as someone else's daughter. You wonder what the fuck happened. How did I raise such an ungrateful *bitch?* That's okay though. There's plenty of hope. You may be particularly distressed because you likely see these attitudes and behaviors directed at you and not necessarily at anyone else. Hence, even if you were to note this to others, they may not even see your perspective because she's kind and gentle with them. For instance, she's having a great time with her siblings at a family gathering, laughing and joking about old times. You walk in to chime in on the conversation and she frowns, folds her arms, and ignores your commentary as if you don't even exist in the room.

Level Four: Oh my—SOS! Maybe you've already thrown in the towel, and this is your last-ditch effort. But please hold on! A few possibilities may be occurring here.

1. Your daughter was deeply betrayed by someone who was influential in her life (e.g., an uncle who molested her) and she never told anyone but blames you for not knowing.
2. She's going through a life phase wherein she doesn't know how to handle it and is taking it out on you because she has security in knowing on some level that you will never abandon her.
3. She's come to realize that she sucked up a lot of hurt she felt during her childhood and now she deeply resents the ways in which she perceives you had failed her but doesn't know how to heal these wounds with you directly.

These are just a few examples of why she is behaving the way she is. Please don't give up yet. Even if you got a high score, that doesn't necessarily mean your daughter is closed off to mending your relationship. She may even be scared of you, or of your reactions if she were to confront you directly by sharing her deepest wounds. So please, at least give all the exercises in this book a chance to work before jumping ship. There are still many more opportunities to come. Hopefully they will allow the door to open to new possibilities.

Now, onward we go so you can have some fun understanding your daughter's subtype. Remember, these exterior mechanisms are meant to serve as protective gear. Even though you may not have perceived creating anything remotely considered dangerous to her survival in the eyes of your daughter, you don't really know how she perceived your actions or intentions. So, as you read the subtypes and the examples below remember that these coping mechanisms were necessary in her mind to get through her own emotional wounds. Also, while some of the characteristics described below may have been the result of emotional wounds in childhood, many may have been inherently present in your daughter from the get-go and simply reinforced by the environment.

So please read on with openness and understanding that these are just a few common types. Your daughter may fit elements of several, or none at all. If these descriptions are not apt to your experience, then try thinking about coming up with a description of your own that does fit. Remember, Rome was not built in a day, nor was your relationship with your adult daughter created in a vacuum. Whatever her age is now is how many years the process has been in the making. Truly, even longer than that because your own relationship to your mother, your mother's relationship to her mother (your grandmother) and on and on, has laid the ground and influenced where you are today with your gal. Also, as noted above, while some of the "who" and the "how" of your daughter has lots to do with the environment and our experiences within it, temperament and other genetic factors certainly also play a significant role. So, toss aside any blame, shame, or judgment toward either yourself or your daughter, no matter how hurt you feel. Instead, hold on to LOVE.

Subtypes of Protective Armor

As with "too nice" moms, a daughter's essence, or even her personality, varies greatly and comes in many different styles, shapes, and forms and could include hundreds of subtypes. For simplicity, however, I've divided them into five subtypes: the *know-it-all*, the *entitled princess*, the *creative genius*, the *indecisive*, and the *D-I-Y gal.* Take a look at these and see if any of them resonate with your experience of your own adult daughter. Of most importance is to note that these protective mechanisms are there to serve a purpose. Ultimately, you will be encouraged to try to understand your daughter and her need to assert these stances from her internal perspective.

The Know-It-All

Let's meet twenty-six-year-old Know-It-All Nancy. Nancy moved away from home at age twenty to pursue her passion for righting the wrongs of the world by attending law school. Nancy's dad left her mom, Ylana, when she was seventeen. From Nancy's perspective, her whole world turned upside down like the aftermath of Black Friday shoppers maniacally rummaging through all the bargain racks in a department store. While she had experienced her parents having high levels of conflict at times, she never anticipated they would sever their relationship, particularly while Nancy and her younger brother were still living at home. From Ylana's perspective (Nancy's mom), Steve (Nancy's dad) bullied her, and she just couldn't take living with him anymore. She truly believed she was protecting her children along with herself so that they wouldn't continually witness an unhealthy intimate relationship dynamic. Nancy, however, viewed her mom as weak and selfish and she carried a grudge. While she saw her mother in a lot of emotional pain and didn't want to add insult to injury by lashing out at her, she secretly blamed her mom for the break-up of the family—a family she largely enjoyed.

Nancy didn't think she could talk to her mother openly about her feelings. So instead, she got through as best she could by focusing even more intensely on her studies, meanwhile continuing to build up a wall between them. Her core protective mechanism became acting like a know-it-all, particularly with regards to her mother.

While it's certainly common for our adult children to think they have all the right answers, they are still usually able to hear another person's points of view and will possibly even modify their viewpoint if the "crazy" adult speaking to them makes some sense. But the know-it-all adult daughter won't budge no matter what information is provided to her, especially if the info is coming from you. Even if you show her evidence of something you're trying to tell her, she'll find a way to dispute it. Why? In Nancy's case, it was because she was angry with her mom, thinking her mom made a wrong decision, and now it was Nancy's job to be the "right" one.

For others, the know-it-all stance may have other roots based in emotional wounds. However, for some it's simply part of the developmental process of distinguishing her identity from yours. Even if she likes things about you, she may simply be compelled to be contrary in order to experience herself as a separate and individuated being from you. Whether you think so or not, she may have felt overwhelmed by your input and is simply trying to assert her own sense of self.

The Entitled Princess

Entitled Emily grew up with two older sisters who were both star athletes. Emily, on the other hand, couldn't toss a ball or balance on one foot if her life depended on it. She was teased a great deal by her sisters who made her feel like a klutz. Though her mom and dad tried to pay equal attention to all three of their much-loved girls, the two older ones commanded more of their parents' attention due to endless practices, games, tournaments, etc. Emily's parents encouraged Emily to find her passions and supported her pursuing them, but Emily mostly loved social activities and playing video games. She was a smart girl but would rather forgo a long study session to get an A if she could have more fun hanging with friends and squeaking by with a B or C. While Emily appeared fairly content on the surface, on a deeper level, she experienced being deprived of the attention she wanted from her parents, and she began acting out in negative ways to get then to notice her more. Simultaneously, she began to exhibit greater levels of entitlement as she approached adulthood, and she primarily targeted her mother for her demands. It was as if her mother owed her a lifetime supply of whatever she wanted because she paid more attention to her siblings; at least through her eyes.

Eventually, once Emily turned twenty-five and demanded that her parents buy her a new car after she'd smashed the last one, her mom, Luanne, stood up to her daughter and said, "NO MORE!" Basically, she set a firm boundary and Emily went ballistic. For sure, they'd had multiple battles along the way, but this one was war, and it took a number of intensive therapeutic interventions to get them onto a positive, mutually respectful playing field.

With this subtype, no matter how much you do for her or give to her, it's never enough. Her hand is always out looking for something else she can take from you. She demands special favors and rarely ever expresses gratitude for your kind gestures. More than likely on some level she felt deprived of something from you. It could be you gave more attention to a sibling (as was Emily's perception) or she's hurt that you weren't able to spend more time with her because your workload at the office was too demanding. You may want to ring her neck at times for being so greedy. Instead, it might be better to try to find and unravel the origin of this defensive posture. Or it's possible that you actually fed the beast too often in her youth and she really has no ability to understand that the world doesn't revolve around her. In any case, children just don't have the same context for understanding a parent's behavior or choices. They just know what feels good and what doesn't. So, if you're dealing with an entitled princess the first place to start is to try to understand how this stance evolved in her.

The Creative Genius

Creative Candace, a thirty-four-year-old photographer, butted heads constantly with her mother, Tina, a sixty-one-year-old physician. While Tina tried to support all of Candace's creative endeavors, a part of her hoped that someday her daughter would grow out of that phase of her life, utilizing the arts as a hobby, not a career. This wasn't that big of a problem between them prior to Candace entering high school, but tension increasingly grew as Tina's expectations of her daughter to get serious about future, stable career options grew. Candace, however, stuck to her passion and continued to pursue her creative spirit through painting, ceramics, and photography. She increasingly found her mother's persistence about her getting serious about her future insulting and demeaning. Tina, however, believed she was simply trying to steer her daughter down a path that would bring her more security. But this was not the way Candace perceived her efforts and she became increasingly "snobby" around her art world and dismissive of her mom.

Like the other examples, this mother and daughter duo grew to fight against each other rather than on the same team and they became polarized to a level of severe dysfunctionality—both feeling unappreciated by the other. Candace began insulting her mother for her values in defense of feeling hurt that her mom did not cherish Candace's artistic talents. Thankfully, once their relationship combusted, they were able to find a way to meet in the middle. One of Tina's fears was that she and her husband would have to support Candace for the rest of their lives, and they didn't want this burden. Tina needed to come to understand that she could give full emotional support to her daughter and allow her daughter to find her own way to make a living, be that via a side job to support her art pursuits or while living on very little until one of her artistic endeavors translated into financial gain. Lo and behold her photography career flourished.

Creative energy can be so powerfully positive and is not something to quell in another being. However, some creatives have a difficult time accepting responsibility for other components more grounded on the Earth; like earning a living or getting a car smog checked. Once these types reach adulthood, they're often resentful that they need to comply with some of the basics of life and may take it out on you. After all, you're the one who nourished all this energy so, "Why are you asking me to get a job?", she might think or say with disdain. The key to this type of dynamic is to support the creative energy but allow yourself not to have to compensate for the other aspects of her life that she needs to also learn to handle on her own.

The Indecisive

Indecisive Inga, a twenty-year-old still living at home with her dad, Bill, and stepmom, Brittany, couldn't make a decision if her life depended on it. Inga's biological mom passed when she was just three years old and her brother, Calvin, just five years old. Bill did the best he could to nurture his children and be there for them, but he had a demanding job, and it had been their mom who predominantly played the caregiver role. Plus, Bill was devastated with feelings of loss, and not knowing how to cope with his grief, he withdrew emotionally. For several years, the siblings were raised by a nanny who wasn't the kindest of beings, and their emotional development suffered as a result. Finally, about three years after the mom's passing, Bill found a lovely lady, Brittany, to whom he proposed and ultimately married when Inga was seven. Brittany brought in a daughter of her own, Julie, age nine at the time, of whom she had joint custody with her ex-husband. While the blending of the families presented many of the usual challenges and conflicts, by and large, the transition went fairly smoothly, and Inga was thrilled to have a mother again.

Over the years, Inga often felt feelings of insecurity and jealousy toward her stepsister and wondered at times whether she was truly loved by Brittany. Her compensation for these fears of inadequacy was to make sure she never made any waves. If she deferred to the others' preferences and desires, then she would be seen as the "easy" one of the bunch and would fly under the radar. The problem, however, was that this became increasingly frustrating to the rest of the family members because they all wanted her to have a voice and participate in family decisions. But none of them were aware of this underlying dynamic with which Inga grappled and she didn't know how to express it.

Over time, both Bill and Brittany became exasperated with how to handle Inga as both grew to perceive her as lazy and apathetic, thereby unknowingly diminishing her sense of self-value even further, to the point she became depressed and withdrawn. Not necessarily clinically depressed, but certainly lacking in joy or passion for life. Plus, because she didn't know how to openly communicate her internal struggle, she often resorted to sarcasm and snide remarks, pushing her loved ones away further and further. Sadly, during one of their family dinners where Inga was consumed in a video game at the table, Brittany blurted out, "Don't you have any respect for us? What's wrong with you?" Unfortunately, while she truly loved Inga as if she were her own daughter, her frustration and sense of powerlessness about what to do for Inga got the best of her and she resorted to a highly shaming remark which she deeply regretted moments after she said it.

On a positive note, this brought the family to therapy and a healing journey unfolded. Inga was able to finally express all the feelings she had buried and learned how to make decisions without fearing the loss of those around her. Brittany learned how to become a more nurturing communicator, thereby appealing to Inga's love language of words of affirmation.

For this type, decision-making can be an excruciatingly painful process, so much so that she just refuses to make one. Buried inside may be a deep fear of losing favor or rocking the boat in a way that might yield dire consequences. The indecisive daughter may continually expect you to make decisions for her, even if she actually knows what she wants. Yet often, once the indecisive reaches puberty and the need for individuation becomes even more pronounced, when you make plans for her, she may get bitchy and rebellious; especially if you made the wrong one. "Jeez, mom, don't you know me better than that?", she might ask with utter annoyance. More than likely, she's plagued by insecurity and doesn't want to disappoint others.

The D-I-Y Gal

Now, let's meet Daphne, the do-it-yourself gal, age thirty-six and mother of three young kids. Daphne grew up as a middle child with an older brother and younger sister. Daphne's mom, Este, worked full-time at a car dealership with rather odd hours, including many weekends. Daphne's dad, Kevin, worked more standard hours, (Monday through Friday) and was often responsible for more of the household chores and the cooking. Both mom and dad loved their children dearly and did their best to spend quality time with their kids, but at the end of the day, quite frankly, there just wasn't enough time and emotional supplies to fill up their children's hearts to the level they desired. Especially since their son suffered attention-deficit disorder. While he was a pretty good kid overall, because of his difficulties staying on task and keeping up in school, he commanded a lot of extra attention and special needs from the parents.

Daphne, a very gentle and empathetic child, inadvertently kept her needs small, so to speak. She certainly didn't want to overwhelm her parents as she could see they had enough on their plates. Her adaptation was to develop a very strong sense of independence and she worked overtime figuring things out for herself so that she would never be perceived as a burden. However, as adolescence hijacked her brain, she began resenting her brother and her parents for their lack of availability. Nevertheless, she forged on, increasingly relying more and more on herself and less on anyone else. Once she became an adult and created her own life as she chose it, her parents, particularly her mom, wanted to make up for lost time and become more involved in her life. On one hand, Daphne wanted to re-open her heart to her mother's offerings, but on the other hand she was afraid something else would take over her mom's attention. She adopted sort of an "it's too little, too late" stance and continually pushed her mother away.

Este, at times, felt like a complete failure as a mom. Her daughter's lack of interest in including her in her life was proof. She didn't realize her daughter was simply holding on to her protective mechanism of total independence because she didn't trust that her mom would understand her feelings. Of course, Daphne wasn't sharing her inner experience. Nevertheless, as is common for many young people, Daphne hoped her mother would figure it out (i.e., be able to read her mind). They were both lost in their own pain and had no idea that these wounds could be healed. Fortunately, Este made the call to me, and her daughter was willing to come to a few sessions. Through rigorous healing practices, both Este and Daphne were able to build a more connected bridge to one another's hearts and their healing ensued.

The D-I-Y type of daughter doesn't want to be told what to do and often won't ask for help no matter how much she may need it. Her sassiness will often show up by means of conveying to you, in one way or another, to mind your own business. She's not really trying to shut you out of her life, but she wants to be in charge of it. She may have perceived the two of you as too close for comfort and she wants to spread her own wings. Possibly, she may have felt smothered, or that she had to adapt to what she believed you needed for her rather than her being able to voice her own needs. Or, like Daphne, she may have felt she needed to rely solely on herself, not perceiving there to be enough emotional supplies for her.

Also, just like with the "too-nice" mom categories, the personality types of sassiness can have overlapping qualities. We just want to aim our focus on those that need the most healing.

Sugar and Spice Exercise:

Take a few moments to consider what type of protective armor your daughter may have erected, using the context of the family in which she was raised as your point of reference. In doing this reflective process, keep in mind that whatever your daughter has erected in her own defense, this safeguarding gear has been meant to hide her own hurt feelings about the ways in which she had yearned for your attention and approval. A daughter looks to her mom to know that she is okay as she is and wants desperately to be honored and cherished in her mother's eyes. No doubt you set out to do just that for her but unfortunately something went awry in either the delivery or the receiving, without any malicious intent. And more than likely, she misperceived many of your actions because she didn't know the full context of your life.

Regardless of your imperfections and the mistakes you've made along the way, you always have the chance to make things better, even if only with yourself. This is a journey of exploration, accountability, acknowledgment, and love—not one of beating yourself up with a sledgehammer. You got this, mama!

Now let's move on for a deeper look at your own imperfections and the challenges you can take on to do your part in the repair process. Remember, we all have imperfections.

CHAPTER 7

Accepting Your Imperfections

If you're like me, it can be very hard to fess up to the ways in which you may have missed the mark while raising your daughter. You hoped you would do a better job than your mom was able to do with you and you wanted her to grow up with confidence, self-esteem, and joie de vivre. You made endless sacrifices to make sure her needs were met, and you showered her with love and affection. Maybe you even hoped she would someday volunteer praise for all the efforts you made to pave the way for her to enjoy a healthy and happy life.

As I shared with you in the introduction, I had a rough time with my own mom, who was a perfectionist. It seemed to me as if I were never good enough in her eyes. But I sure did try! As an example, when I was about twelve years old, I had saved up $30 (about $200.00 equivalency today) so I could buy her a piece of jewelry for her birthday. I would forgo weekends of playtime with friends to be the helper at my parents' parties, serving hors d'oeuvres and cleaning up dishes until the wee hours of the night, just to win my mom's approval. (Granted she did pay me $1.00 per hour, which would be worth about $7.00 per hour today). But, no matter what I tried, the criticisms flowed out of her like the Mississippi River streaming into the Gulf of Mexico.

Sadly, it took me decades to realize that my mom believed she was showing me love but she just couldn't do it in a way that ever felt very loving to me. That's not to say that she didn't have a few vulnerable moments where I could feel her love. Sometimes she would even call me "darling," causing my heart to melt like butter on freshly popped popcorn. But these moments were often short-lived as she would inevitably become irritated by something someone had done or not done, and then become critical and harsh. For instance, if I'd left a cup of water on the coffee table while getting ready for bed, she could spiral into a rant about how messy and untidy I was. Eventually, I learned that her childhood was certainly no picnic, filled with violence and neglect, leaving her with a deeply wounded inner child.

Over time and through my studies and work as a psychologist, I finally came to understand that no matter how much I felt my mom had hurt me along the way, she was really doing the best she could with the limited internal resources she had. She couldn't truly show love and acceptance to me because she never healed her internalized pain. Hence, she continued the generational cycle of dysfunction.

My Journey with My Daughter

Naturally, I wanted more than ever for my daughter, Tiffany, to feel loved and accepted in a way that I had rarely felt. However, although I thought I had done a great deal of personal growth work prior to becoming a parent, I soon learned that my own internal resources were also limited. Hence, I was practicing my parental role while simultaneously healing from my own childhood wounds. And unfortunately, no matter what my best of intentions were, my own internal struggles prohibited me at times from being the mom I so eagerly wanted to be. There were many times I wasn't there for my girl in the way she needed me to be. At one point I would joke with her, letting her know that not only was I saving for her college fund, but also for her psychotherapy fund.

While I believe I made every effort available to keep the lines of communication open with my daughter to share with me in real time her feelings, disappointments, etc., I now know I didn't make it entirely safe for her to be as candid as I had hoped. Tiffany, being such a caring and giving soul herself, didn't want to hurt my feelings. While my mother would have raged at me if I ever complained, I was more of the mush pile of sadness, guilt, and shame. So, while I thought I was a tough enough cookie and could hear it all, I guess I didn't hide my sensitivity well enough, and she took it upon herself to protect me.

I share this with you to let you know that you are not alone on this journey. To help deepen the meaning of this book, I asked Tiffany several questions regarding her own emotional wounds stemming from our relationship.

Through Tiffany's answers to the questions, I learned several things. Some of these I had been completely unaware of, such as her struggles in a variety of areas, including those around the process of menstruation, body image, and her sexuality. I also came to realize that while I had thought her dad and I had done a pretty darn good job in developing an amicable co-parenting relationship after our divorce, when Tiffany was quite young, I hadn't realized some of the subtle, yet profound, effects this had on her development of an inner sense of security. Not to mention, I had made a few very poor choices in intimate partners, leaving her without a great road map for navigating healthy love relationships.

Something she wrote that made me particularly sad was learning that she struggled with a mild eating disorder. Here's what she had to say: "I'm not sure if my mom realized that I really did have a (relatively mild) eating disorder. It was tied up with body image and I struggled internally for a while. I never wanted to fully admit that to my mother because I know that she had such a hard time with her eating disorder in her youth and never wanted to pass that on to me. I want to acknowledge my mom for how much she did to foster a healthier relationship to food/body image than I know she had growing up (which was terrible). So, the generational wound has definitely softened and healed in many ways, and I feel I have a healthy relationship with food now. I guess I felt like I couldn't share because I knew she would take it personally as a reflection on her. I felt afraid to hurt her feelings, because I know how hard she tries and that she really cares and loves me. But in the spirit of being very honest, I do wish that I could have told her, because it was a hard time in my life where I really felt a lot of self-hatred and would swing through starvation and bingeing." While she was right in that I would likely have felt bad to know she suffered in this way, I wish I could have been there for her through those struggles.

I also learned that she missed me a lot due to my being a working mom, even though she pretended to be so self-sufficient as an only child, the D-I-Y type. Had I practiced better self-care, I would have spent more quality and quantity time with Tiffany. It's taken me a long time to fully integrate the importance of self-care, even though I've been coaching others in this arena for decades. Finding a balance between work and family time was sometimes quite a struggle but I regret not having made more time for her.

Below are a few more excerpts from Tiffany's answers to my query about how I missed the mark in parenting her and how to be instrumental in her healing:

"I cannot expect my mom to rewrite the past, and I also have to acknowledge that it's ultimately my work now to help my inner child feel loved, safe, and whole. However, the support from my mother is greatly welcomed and adds a beautiful balm to the wounds. Healing requires us to hold space for the full spectrum of our beings, bring to the light of consciousness what we try to hide in the dark, feel and express our emotions, and take new healthy actions moving forth. Being able to share these things openly with her now, and feeling her receptivity is healing in itself. I feel that she genuinely wants to look at her mistakes, take ownership, and use the pain as compost for new seeds."

She continued to so wisely offer, "I think something that stops the healing process is wanting to pretend like it's all okay or to jump to forgiveness before we're ready. I'm realizing that I am often afraid to hurt my mom's feelings, and I don't want to be angry at her or resent her, and I know how precious her heart is. But I also need to not gloss over my true feelings. So, I think the more she can continue to welcome my truth and feel it with me, the more healing happens."

She further added, "Maybe it's okay that I can feel hurt and be angry at my mother for the places she messed up. Maybe I don't have to rush the process of forgiveness or pretend like the scars aren't there. Because the truth is that a scar is a scar; we can rub oil on it, soothe it with herbs, and maybe it will fade or soften a bit, but it still stays with us, and it holds its story. It's a story that we can learn from and use as a reminder for how to do better next time. For me, the deepest healing is in the soul-felt knowing that my mother is here with me, not just on the surface, but in the depths of her core—to know I'm not alone. It's in the trust that I can let myself cry and melt into that soft space of vulnerability with all of the shit and all of the pain and all of the unresolved whatever, and she can just be there with tears in her eyes and an 'I'm sorry' in heart and big open arms to hold me in that wordless space of mother's love. Maybe we can both heal in this embrace as the ancestral knots loosen, and our traumas turn to tears that can water the soil of a new garden for the children to come."

The Ouch Response

When I first read Tiffany's answers, I experienced a deep sadness in my heart. I felt so bad that she had been carrying these wounds with her and I desperately wanted to explain and defend myself. However, that's not what she needed. Rather, she needed me to acknowledge that these are the ways in which *she* processed the world I created for her and for me to be there for her in her emotional pain. Of course, her internalized perceptions and interpretations of my actions left me with pangs of guilt and wishing I could erase some of the past. But we all know this is not possible and beating myself up wouldn't change anything. She is a very brave young woman to share all of this with me and to allow me to share this with you. So, I, too, had to be brave enough to hold space for her pain and recognize that I was a part of it.

What helps a lot, though, is also knowing the things our daughters truly cherish about us as their mother—thereby soothing some of the "ouch" response. Here's what Tiffany had to say: "I am deeply grateful for my mother's capacity to want to heal and grow. Even throughout our rocky journey over the years (especially as a teen), we would always find a way to talk through our challenges and come back to connection. She always encouraged me to be open with her and so I always felt I had a safe place to talk, and I didn't feel like I needed to hide things. I never felt afraid that I might be punished for something I'd done or tried; even if it wasn't something to be proud of, my mother didn't judge me. She allowed me to be me. 🙏

I love my mother's fun and playful spirit. The moments where she is exuberant with joy sometimes at the littlest things. She has a way of lighting up a room with her excitement, sometimes seeming to be having way more fun than anyone else in the room, spreading her adorable, childlike spirit in such a way that you cannot help but laugh and smile right along with her.

I love my mother's capacity to carry out deep, meaningful conversations. We have had such beautiful talks about so many facets of life, and it's always such a treat to connect with her in this way. This also goes in line with her incredibly kind and empathetic heart. She is always able to hold me when I'm going through something challenging or I need to talk; she can really feel and relate to me in a way that makes me feel validated, safe, loved, and supported even through the darkest moments.

I love you, Mom. 🖤"

So, while the initial ouch response can truly sting and may generate a response of, "but you...," when it comes time to asking for feedback from your daughter, you'll need to seriously refrain from the knee jerk reaction of defending or explaining yourself. And hopefully, her also sharing about the things she cherishes about you will help soothe your potential "ouch" response and give you the strength to face your imperfections (as she sees them) head on.

Acknowledging Our Own Imperfections

No one, and I mean no one, has had the "ideal" childhood, despite a caregiver's good intentions. Raising a child is a work in progress, ever evolving and changing along the way. And, if you went through trauma such as abuse, neglect, severe loss, or endured a cataclysmic catastrophe, the picture can be very bleak and increase the likelihood that you passed along some of these wounds to your children. Plus, your children may have also passed along some emotional scars to their own children, if they have any yet. Nevertheless, we can lessen this burden of generational trauma by identifying our issues and owning our responsibility and the impact these had on our daughters at any point in the life cycle.

Acknowledging our imperfections is no easy task and can become even more challenging if we are mired in shame and guilt; two states of being that cloud our ability to look at things clearly. Though people often use these words interchangeably, these experiences are different enough to warrant further explanation. Shame is the experience of I *am* bad, unlovable, undeserving, etc., whereas guilt is the experience of I *behaved* badly but my "self" is still intact. Both experiences can lead us into denial or some other defense mechanism to avoid the pain of observing our own behavior, especially through our daughter's eyes. However, shame, more so than guilt, creates the biggest obstacle we face in acknowledging our imperfections and in keeping a dialogue open for healing. So, more than ever, we need to heal our own shame and learn from our mistakes.

Some shame-based people wear their shame on their sleeve. They outwardly put themselves down, avoid relationships for fear of being rejected or discovered for how flawed they are, or they make themselves invisible. Others, however, carry their shame unconsciously but it still leaks out in various ways such as by becoming excessively controlling, blaming others for one's own mistakes or limitation, or needing people to deny their reality. Essentially, shame interferes with one's ability to face and accept what's actually so and to take responsibility for one's own actions. Excessive guilt can have the same negative impact, though usually less intensely. In either case, shame and guilt, in small doses, can serve to motivate oneself to make positive changes and correct mistakes, but when imposed on the self like a sledgehammer used to demolish a perfectly good structure that only needed a few repairs, these states of being will wreak havoc on our relationship with ourselves and others.

Sugar and Spice Exercise:

Here's an opportunity to take a serious look at how you were raised and whether you are ridden with shame. Ask yourself the following questions and be as candid as possible with your answers.

1. Were any of your influential caregivers afflicted with either shame or guilt or both?
2. Was either shame or guilt, or both, used as a parenting tool in your family of origin?
3. If so, what do you recall as your personal experiences of feeling shame and guilt?
4. Did you resort to this approach with your daughter?
5. How do you think shame and guilt affect you today?

Once you've done this exercise, spend some time with your answers to truly discover if you have any shame or guilt holes affecting your ability to be receptive to your daughter's feedback on your parenting of her. And then write a letter of forgiveness to yourself for all of the self-deprecating things you have done. Find a picture of yourself as a little girl and promise her that you will do all you can from today forward to practice self-love and acceptance. Try this several times for the next few weeks to create space within yourself to see your imperfections.

If you have difficulty letting go of shame and guilt, you may need to take a detour for a bit and work on healing in this way first. However, since this is a tough love guide for improving your relationship with your daughter, not necessarily a nurturing self-repair kit, I can't spend too much more time on providing these tools here. Nevertheless, that doesn't mean you shouldn't continue reading on, but you will need more self-support than is currently available in this book. There is much written on this topic, so please find a book or a meditation on healing shame. You might also try my book *Healing the Sensitive Heart* (available through my website as a PDF.)

Once you feel you can look at yourself with a solid sense of feeling okay, then make a list of the ways in which you wished you had been a better parent. Try to perceive yourself through your daughter's eyes, if possible. By now she has probably given you some harsh criticisms along the way, desperately hoping that you could see things from her point of view. The goal here is to create a loving space within yourself to truly observe your own imperfections without shame, guilt, or blame and eventually be able to fess up to your daughter.

In the next chapter, you'll learn how to make amends and create a healing tree with your girl. Also note that at the end of the book, you'll find samples of other brave women who shared their experiences with their moms to help you further along with how to process the information you receive. Even if you opt out of asking for your daughter's feedback because you're just not ready, or you think she might be cruel or harsh toward you, you may still benefit from reviewing what others have written and the process of how to continue the healing.

CHAPTER 8

Making Amends and Planting a Healing Tree

Now that you've been building a foundation of better self-love, ridding yourself of shame and guilt, and accepting your imperfections with grace, you have a fresh opportunity to make amends and plant the seeds for a healing tree with your daughter. Ideally, this tree will grow, thrive, be enjoyed, and ultimately passed down to future mother—daughter bonds. However, because your daughter will need to provide some of her own fertile soil, there is no way to guarantee that she will accept your gestures. Hence, you may try all, or many, of the recommended methods below and throughout the book to no avail. Nevertheless, so long as you're doing your part, at the very least you will know deep in your heart that you gave your daughter your best efforts. And, if your daughter continues to remain unreceptive, you can work toward letting go and allowing her the time and space to hopefully come around some day. But for now, I encourage you to keep on trying.

Extending the Olive Branch

In my experience, more often than not, people soften in their hearts when offered an olive branch (i.e., a gesture of peace and goodwill). However, this can still prove to be a very delicate process, especially with regards to healing wounds with your adult daughter and one that will require some advance thinking and planning. To facilitate this process for you, below you'll find some guidelines for how to begin the process of inviting your daughter to engage in this healing process with you. First and foremost, you need to get into the mindset that you are extending a loving invitation for her to heal, with you, the wounds she has perceived you to be responsible for creating. I know, you might be thinking, "But what about all the sassy and rude things she has said or done to me? When do I get my time to say what I feel and think?" These are valid questions and concerns. The answer is both you will, and you won't. In other words, the process will probably look different than you imagine. While there will be opportunities for you to share from your perspective, if you jump the gun, looking for reciprocity at this point, your efforts will likely backfire.

Also, please note I'm not at all asking you to put yourself in harm's way or open yourself up to abuse. If your daughter suffers from any sort of mental health issues such as a personality disorder (e.g., narcissistic or borderline personality disorder) or bipolar disorder, the suggestions that follow may not be appropriate. If you have reason to suspect that the difficulties in your relationship extend beyond unhealed emotional wounds and the resulting protective shields, then before embarking on the path outlined here you may want to first seek professional counseling and advice. Otherwise, let's get started with your olive branch.

Sugar and Spice Exercise: Creating the Seeds

Before approaching your daughter, we need to first find the seeds you wish to plant. Much of how you ultimately decide to approach your daughter will be determined by the specifics of your situation with her (e.g., where she lives, how much you perceive she'll be receptive, her current life conditions and complications, etc.). So please do a thorough analysis of what you believe to be the best option for you. Assuming you are still on some speaking terms with your girl, then I recommend this be as personable as possible.

Before you actually reach out to her, it can often be valuable to journal a free flow of all your thoughts and feelings, including any resentments you may hold toward her. Here is your chance to air out your own upsets—but this piece of writing will NOT be shared with your daughter. I believe as you gain a new perspective and get honest feedback from your daughter (ideally not from her protective guard), your own container of hurt and resentment will start to dissipate. Hence, you'll be less inclined to have to defend or explain yourself. Wouldn't that be nice! So, for this exercise—go full throttle.

Once you feel you have reaped the benefits of a cathartic cleanse for yourself, then you can move on to what you will decide to express directly to your gal. When ready, please take some time to write out what you would like to say to her to plant the seeds of the healing tree. Here is an example:

Dearest (name of your daughter),

I love you with all my heart. I hope you know that I've done the best I can and have always had good intentions while raising you. But I don't know that I've ever really stopped long enough to invite you to truly share with me any childhood wounds you may be carrying around with you after all these years. More than anything, I want you to know I would like to be part of your healing journey. I want to be receptive to hearing your feedback regarding how I parented you and how I can help heal your inner child. (Note: some people reject the notion of an inner child. If you believe your daughter is among that camp you might try another word or phrase, such as "the hurt little girl in you," "your more vulnerable side," "that part of you that carries hurt from long ago," or "the parts of you behind your strong exterior," etc. You may be angry with me for things I've done, or maybe you have hidden your deepest concerns for fear of hurting my feelings or having me lash out at you in blame or accusation. I've been doing some deep inner work myself and believe I am now secure enough to be able to take in your candid feedback. I know I've made many mistakes. (You might name a few here, if it feels right.) And I want to repair these wounds. I want us to have the best relationship possible and want to do my part in making things better between us. I believe this will be an ongoing process, possibly taking quite some time to do this healing work. I am up for the challenge. Are you? If so, I'd love to send you a series of questions. Your answers to them will give me better insight into your own internal process. I would be ever so grateful to know more about you!

Love always and deeply, Mom

I recommend you send your message via email or as a hand-written letter to her. The written word can be so powerful and something to be referred to over and over, especially if someone feels doubtful about what was actually said. I also suggest you let her know via voicemail, phone/video chat, or text message that she will be receiving a letter from you that is heart-felt and extremely meaningful to you and that you hope she will carve out time to truly allow herself to let your message sink in. Please note, it's best to try to also be sensitive to the timing of all this, particularly if this is the first time you are embarking on this type of journey. For example, it is probably not a good idea if she is about to deliver a baby or if she is leaving for her dream vacation for which she has saved every penny. Then again, there could be big life events coming up for her and knowing that you want to heal with her could be the most supportive and welcoming gift of a lifetime. So, give this some thought and maybe ask someone in your inner circle who has a good take on your daughter whether your timing is appropriate.

Once you deliver your message to your daughter, take a pause and give her ample time and space to respond. If she doesn't respond to your letter at all (maybe after a couple of weeks), check in with her to make sure she received it. If she says she hasn't, then of course you can resend it. But if she says she has and doesn't say anymore, you can poke her just a little bit and ask her if she intends to respond and what she believes is a reasonable timeline. If she ignores you completely, though, you're going to have to back off. I certainly hope that will not be the case.

If she does respond favorably, and you feel ready for the next step, then invite your daughter to answer the six-item questionnaire below. By the way, these are the actual questions I asked my daughter to answer. Also, you can find several other daughters' responses to these questions at the end of the book.

1. What do you wish I would have known about you during your teens (or anytime in your life for that matter), but you were afraid to ask/tell me? (e.g., you had an abortion, you tried a drug, you skipped school, etc.)
2. What are the top three emotional wounds (or more if you'd like) you are still carrying around with you that you blame on me?
3. What can I do to heal these wounds?
4. What are the top three characteristics that annoy you most about me and wish I would change?

5. What are the top three things you cherish about me, and hope will never change? (After all—moms need gratitude too!)
6. If you could name anything you wish I would do for you now, what would it be? (On this one, I ask you to please refrain from naming material objects for me to purchase for you and instead focus on what I can provide for you emotionally.)

Feel free to modify these questions anyway you like. Or you may not want to send anything just yet as you may need more time to fully process what you discover about your own history and how it continues to affect you. And that's totally fine. There is no time pressure in this process. You want to be in the most grounded place possible before you get candid feedback from your girl.

If you do decide to ask for your daughter's feedback, set the stage by reminding her of the following:

- Your goal is to help you be able to begin a healing journey with her.
- This is a process of love and hope.
- Encourage her to be open and candid but to also be kind in her responses.
- Remind her that you won't necessarily agree with all her perceptions (it's easy to rewrite history) but you will do all you can to hold space for her perspective and her resulting interpretations and feelings.

Sugar and Spice Exercise: Planting the Seeds

Whatever feedback you receive from your daughter, be super careful to stay open-hearted to understanding *her* experience without minimizing, deflecting, denying, explaining, or defending yourself. Note, you will be encouraged later to invite your daughter to hear from you about your experience and the things she may not have known about you, just not quite yet. Let her know you truly want to learn about her internal suffering. Imagine if your mother had made that openness available to you. The key here is to put aside the desire to correct your daughter. Her perception of things may be a bit skewed. For instance, I recall many days where Tiffany and I would spend lots of quality time together, making cookies or dinner, playing games, etc. But what she expressed instead was, "I would sometimes envy my friends who had stay-at-home moms, going to their house after school and having her prepare snacks... simple little things that just felt homey and sweet. I often felt a sense of my mom being on the go, like she always had something to do, and I wanted more grounded presence and time with her."

So even though I thought I was spending ample time doing sweet things with her, it didn't register as enough for her. Mind you, on some of the things my daughter stated I don't know that I could have done things much differently because of varying degrees of responsibilities I held outside of raising her. But, on several occasions I would certainly have done things differently had I been better healed myself, especially in the realm of wishing I had made better choices in relational partners. But that's also another book.

The point is that you will likely have very reasonable explanations as to why you did things the way you did. And between you and me—those explanations may be rock solid. But I think if you dig deeply enough, you may find that some of your choices, decisions, and actions with your daughter may have been wound-driven (i.e., pressured by some of your own unhealed childhood or even adult emotional bruises). So, before you become quick to defend, even in your own mind, take a long pause and reflect on how or why she drew the conclusions she did.

Please ask her to be as candid as possible while simultaneously being kind in her delivery. Let her know to take her time and if she's unable to share it with you now to let you know when she feels ready. Tell her that you will not punish her emotionally for her responses and that you will take the time necessary to digest what she has disclosed. Ultimately, you want to be able to express empathy for her experience without justifying, making excuses, or even explaining at this phase of healing.

It may be hard to imagine at this point that the feedback you receive (or have already received) from your daughter will ultimately be one of the greatest gifts of a lifetime, especially if she were able to voice herself with kindness and compassion. In my experience, if a child (in this case your adult daughter) is angry and hurt, she will usually soften when offered an open heart and empathetic ear. While at first the feedback may feel like being stung by a swarm of bees and then puffing up like a blowfish, ultimately the information is like a beautiful rose blossoming, even though its thorns remain sharp.

Keep in mind, this process will likely take some time, and a great deal of patience on your part. Both of you will likely have to get over defensiveness and protectiveness and instead build a safety net of trust and a genuine desire to heal and repair. You may encounter a lot of tears and misunderstandings. Your daughter may lash out at you wherein you will need to set some healthy and loving limits with her. Hopefully, all the while, you're both inching your way toward more loving, respectful, and open communication.

Sugar and Spice Exercise: Growing the Tree

Fertilizing the Soil Seeds: Below are my top seven recommendations on how to fertilize the ground to potentially have the highest chance of growing a strong and resilient healing tree.

1. *Be empathetic.* Empathy doesn't necessarily imply agreement. Two people can share different points of view or even memories of the same event. But that doesn't prohibit the ability to put yourself in your daughter's shoes and see an event through her eyes. After all, it is what *she* observed, how *she* interpreted it, and then how *she* felt about it. So even if things didn't happen in your memory the way she described it, you can still empathize with her feelings. She couldn't see your *intentions*, only your actions. We've all felt the myriad of basic emotions from sad to glad and from afraid to mad along with all the other fancy combinations (rage, frustration, confusion, etc.). So, all you need to do is draw upon an experience in your life wherein you felt an emotion your daughter has expressed and share that you understand how she feels (insert feeling here). Keep in mind that people often disguise their thoughts (opinions, judgments, criticisms, observations, etc.) as feelings. So, make sure you understand her feelings.

2. *Be patient.* It's not easy for anyone to wait for something one may want so badly! You're not alone if you have difficulty staying the course and not rushing the process. Also, it's quite likely that your daughter has not entered on her own path of healing, let alone with you, and she may have to catch up, or even first find the value in doing so.

3. *Be kind.* Consider the delicateness of this journey for both of you. We generate kindness by staying in our hearts as opposed to living too much in our heads. Our hearts bring love, and then kindness easily follows.

4. *Be open-minded.* All of us can become very rigid in our mindset. We become convinced that our own perception is the one

that's accurate if someone else disagrees. Sometimes it's valuable to be headstrong and righteous, but not in this context. You want to come from a place of learning more deeply about your daughter's experience of you. You're not on this journey to convince her that everyone else on the planet who has met you thinks you're great. Instead, you're here to find out how you can win back her heart and for her to trust that you are a safe person for her to come to.

5. *Refrain from defending.* If you're prone to becoming defensive, you may have some underlying guilt or shame about something your daughter discloses to you. So, practice reminding yourself over and over that you are a good person even if you misread or misunderstood your daughter and her needs. Again, providing a context for your daughter through explanation will come down the line, just not quite yet.

6. *Gauge how much to share.* If your daughter shows interest in learning more about you and the context in which certain events occurred, that's awesome. Nevertheless, check in with her on a regular basis as to how much she's willing to hear. In my experience, the deeper the empathy, the more she'll feel understood and heard, and her own empathetic heart may start to re-emerge.

7. *Keep trying.* As long as you see small bits of progress, keep trying. If you're not seeing any progress, you may want to revisit whether you're actually practicing items 1–6, or you may need a horticulturist!

Making Amends

Below is a nine-step recipe guide on how to make amends with your adult daughter once you've received her feedback.

Step One:

Make a list of all the things you've discovered about yourself as a mom and the wounds you may have carried forward into your parenting approach and style. Write out all of these in the most heartfelt and self-loving way possible.

Step Two:

Own up to the mistakes you've made and promises or agreements you believe you can make going forward to try to be different in your interactions with your daughter. Take your time with this. If she's been able or willing to provide you with the answers to your questions you can work off her material. If not, take an honest look at yourself and create your own answers, letting her know that she is free to correct you or fill in if you have a misunderstanding of that which may be the undercurrent for her current attitude.

Step Three:

Ask your daughter to talk to you about all of these items and encourage her to share even more deeply by asking yet more curious questions. This will help you stay in the discovery mode rather than jumping too quickly into explaining yourself. Your job at this phase is to listen empathetically, not needing to correct her misperceptions of you, but simply to acknowledge, one after the other, her experiences and her resulting feelings.

Step Four:

Ask for her forgiveness. Note: Forgiveness is often taught as something we give to someone regardless of their behavior or acknowledgement of any wrongdoing. I actually disagree. To be able to forgive someone means that someone needs to acknowledge her mistake and the hurt her actions may have created, even if having come from the best of intentions. But we can let go of something that someone *hasn't* fessed up to and taken responsibility for. In this process with my daughter, Tiffany set up a Whatsapp chat for the two of us which we named, *The Healing Tree*. We created this space so that I could have a place to share my empathy, regrets, and understanding of her wounds and where she could respond. This allowed us to have sacred space uncluttered with the day-to-day chit chat. It's really cool! Find a forum that works for the two of you.

Step Five:

Aside from ideally receiving forgiveness from your daughter, you absolutely must also ask yourself for forgiveness. We've all made mistakes and have had cases of poor judgment. Having limitations and imperfections makes us human. But if we always need to portray ourselves as "right" or without flaws, we become unapproachable and unable to enjoy truly healthy close bonds with others. Do your own personal inventory and give yourself compassion and understanding.

Step Six:

Define with each other what it would take for a brighter future together. Talk to her about how to move through the past and create a new and healthy bond in the present. Let her know that you need her input. Be as specific as possible. For instance, instead of global statements like, "Let's just be kinder to one another", agree to something more like, "If one of us gets our feelings hurt, they to tell the other within (name the period of time), so the other doesn't have to be a mind-reader."

Step Seven:

Create a plan for how to make things better in the present and future and define the steps you will each take if the plan isn't working. For instance, if one of the things she wanted was to be able to talk to you more frequently, but you've been too busy at work or have made most of the conversations about your own woes in life, set up a reasonable frequency for connection. If it turns out that either of you cannot meet the agreement or would like it to be even more frequent, modify the agreement.

Step Eight:

Gather her permission to share the context in which you made the choices you made in parenting her. Finally, here's your opportunity to provide context. Keep in mind that your daughter may still need more one-sided empathy and time to witness changes in you before she's open to a more reciprocal exchange. But generally, as I've already pointed out, most people usually open their heart once they feel understood. Just think of how wonderful and vindicating it would have been had your mother ever said the words, "I'm sorry honey, I see that what I did made you sad. And in hindsight, I wish I had done that differently!" I know I certainly wished I had heard my mother say something to that effect. Wouldn't you?

Step Nine:

Establish loving boundaries with one another regarding personal space and involvement in one another's lives. You'll find tips on this later in Chapter Twelve.

CHAPTER 9

Some Things are Best Kept Private

Whether you've started the healing process or not, it's good to get a little perspective on what to share versus what's best kept private. Should I tell her everything I discover about myself during this healing process? Have I done something so horrible that she may never forgive me? What if I remember something, but she doesn't? Do I disclose? All these questions and more may come to mind. After all, this is a very slow and delicate process.

While I can't give you a step-by-step roadmap on what to share or not to share, let me try to address the general question of how much and what to share by presenting to you even more questions, and a few examples, using two main markers: life before daughter and life after daughter.

Life Before Daughter:

You have your history. We all do. Did you have sex with random guys, possibly having been considered promiscuous by your friends? Did you look for love in all the wrong places with all the wrong people? Or were you that someone who waited for the "one"? Did you experiment with a lot of drugs? Were you ever raped or molested? Were your parents neglectful or abusive? Did you steal something from a store on a dare from your friends? Did you ditch school? Did you do things you regretted but then tried to protect your image by portraying yourself as "saintlier" than you were? Were you selling to yourself that you had to shelter your daughter from your own mistakes? What does your daughter know about you already? These are the types of questions I suggest you ask yourself.

You may now be feeling like you want to tell your daughter everything. Or you may be in the place of, "What the fuck! Was I so screwed up and unhealed that I made a mess out of my daughter's psyche? Did I do anything right, or did I do everything wrong?" Again, being on a healing path can be very challenging and bring up a lot of doubt and defense mechanisms to protect yourself from feeling bad. But remember, you are not on this journey for self-pity or self-deprecation. This is all about learning and growing and being able to bring new ingredients to the mix with your gal, and ultimately helping to foster a new and improved relationship with her.

So, what do you share about your life pre-daughter? The answer; whatever you think would give your daughter context about you so that she can see you in a three-dimensional way. You're not just a story or a bunch of photos. You're a live woman who is also the daughter of a mother. You have a lineage and legacy. However, having said that, keep in mind that your daughter is your ultimate gauge. Would she benefit from your sharing, or is it more self-serving to make a case for the mistakes you may have made as her mother?

Basically, you need to enlist her feedback about how much she truly cares to know. She may already have a reservoir of information that was leaked out here and there, but she may not know specific relevant details because she was too young to handle certain material. Or, while she was developing, you may have shared more than she cared to know because you looked to her for nurturance and forgiveness. She may even have some unspoken resentment about having felt she needed to nurture or "mother" you while growing up to protect you from your own pain.

Let's meet Paulina, a fifty-three-year-old former bartender, and her daughter, Jessie, a tech support member of a small software company in her mid-twenties. Paulina had quite the life pre-daughter. She had multiple sexual partners and periodically engaged in experimentation with drugs; cannabis mostly, but also cocaine and ecstasy. During her twenties, she was uncertain about her sexuality and explored both bisexual encounters and polyamorous relationships. Ultimately, though, she met Frank, with whom she fell in love and decided to try to commit to the traditional monogamous relationship with him. Sadly, neither Frank nor Paulina could fulfill their promises of fidelity and they ultimately divorced when Jessie was twelve and her brother eight.

During their marriage both cheated on each other; Paulina seeking women on the side and Frank having turned to porn for extracurricular entertainment. Jessie observed her parents' unhappiness and it weighed on her heavily. Her parents did not have an amicable divorce. To the contrary, it was quite contentious. Jessie knew very little of her mother's history and over the years, and as she entered adulthood, she wanted to know more about her mother's past. But Paulina was too ashamed of what she came to perceive as poor choices and painted a much "purer" picture of herself to her daughter.

As it turns out, Paulina's parents were exceptionally permissive, setting virtually no boundaries for her. She had the freedom to do whatever she wanted, whenever. By the time she was twenty-one she'd had at least thirty sexual partners, some consensual and some not really. Some might have been considered rape—but she was often on mind-altering substances which made her memory rather fuzzy as to whether she wanted the sex or not.

Paulina kept most of what she considered to be a sordid past to herself except for a few friends she entrusted and a previous therapist she'd sought counsel from in her late twenties. She had shared some of what she considered to be shameful secrets with Frank, but mostly spared him the details. But for the most part, Jessie was left in the dark.

Jessie was often curious about her mother's history. She had the sense that her mother wasn't the "goodie two shoes" she portrayed herself to be. However, like for many daughters, Jessie thought she wanted to know the scoop. Yet she really didn't have the capacity, or the maturity, to integrate the details. For her, inquiring minds really didn't want to know. However, as Jessie got older, she truly did want more truth from her mother. Paulina was stunned when she came to see me. She asked with great concern, "What should I actually disclose?"

As our work together unfolded, it was clear that Paulina needed to process and heal the shame she carried from her childhood. She'd gone into a twelve-step program for substance abuse and had cleaned up her act. However, she hadn't really dealt with the traumas she'd experienced along the way, many of which had led her to act out. She had been raped as a young teenager and her parents had been emotionally abusive. She sought out older boys, even men, to soothe her pain and drugs came along with the package.

Once she decided on the path of marriage, she tried to fit a stereotypic middle-class mold, becoming the girl scout troop volunteer and the soccer mom, but even though she did her best, her trauma informed much of her decision making. She tried to hide the behaviors she had decided were unacceptable from her children, but they knew something wasn't matching up. Especially

Jessie. When Jessie was fourteen and she began asking more and more detailed questions, Paulina knew it wasn't really the time to bare the whole truth. It would have been too much information. Once Jessie was an adult and Paulina had done more healing work on herself, it was time to open up more about her history and validate for Jessie some of her intuitive knowing that her mother had a much more complicated history than had appeared on the surface.

While Paulina's story may be more intense than your situation, it's a great example of how challenging it can be to decipher what's just the right quantity or quality of disclosure. It illuminates the tricky balance of what to share and what's best kept private.

Like Paulina, and all mothers and daughters, we all had our past. Some of our memories we cherish and some we feel ashamed of. We may feel compelled to do a full disclosure in this process, believing our daughters would want to know everything about us. Or, we may want to earn her sympathy, convincing ourselves that if she knew the gory details about our hardships and the resulting woes we suffered, she would be more forgiving. Sort of like purging our conscience.

Crystal, a forty-two-year-old mother, was sending her daughter, Alicia (eighteen years old), off to college when her daughter asked her how many guys her mom had sex with before she got married to Alicia's dad. Alicia also asked her mom what drugs she'd tried in her life. Crystal was a bit taken aback and had no idea how to answer the questions. Crystal had several sexual experiences before meeting her future husband, Tony, but couldn't see the relevance to Alicia's life. She'd also tried her fair share of illegal substances, but she didn't want her daughter to know. Being tongue-tied and feeling self-conscious and embarrassed, Crystal said, "Not sure those are topics I want to share with you." Alicia shut down and felt super hurt because she was trying to gauge what was normal. She'd wanted to talk to her mom about her sexuality and other stuff for years, but she didn't think her mom would be available for such candid conversations. So, when she finally tested the waters, her fears were confirmed. Her mom thought she was trying to protect her daughter, when in truth she was trying to protect the image her daughter had of her as a "good girl."

Regina, mother of Roxanne (twenty-two), when asked a similar question launched into a full-fledged explosion of her entire sexual history and drug experimentation, believing her daughter would see her as the "cool" mom. Unfortunately, her verbal diarrhea backfired. Roxanne, who really seemed intrigued and claimed to want to know all the details of her mother's past, later suffered some distress and anxiety. She thought she was mature enough to handle the information, but it actually tainted her image of her mother, leading her to perceive and judge her mom as overly indulgent.

While airing your dirty laundry may feel good in the short run, the question is—does it have any long-term benefits to your relationship with your grown daughter? And how much is too much? I can't really give you specific guidance because each person is very different. Just like in some marriages where a partner has cheated, the cheated may want all the information, whereas others don't want to know any specifics because they don't want to feel haunted by the imagery. So, this will truly come down to what you and your daughter decide.

Life As a Mother

Many of us make significant changes in our lives once we embrace the role of motherhood. We have a fresh start at building a bond with a new little being, ideally attempting to replicate that which we saw as good from our relationship with our own mothers and to fix that which we thought was broken. We try to correct behaviors we may view as unbecoming of a loving mother. Plus, we hope our children will see us in a positive light and find our hearts to be enormously nourishing and fulfilling.

Naturally, you want to put your best foot forward and have her see all the good stuff in you. But you're human and you have foibles and imperfections, and you will not have been able to camouflage all of these "darker" sides. Children are very observant, and they can often see what we try so hard to hide.

Now your daughter is a grown woman. Again, the question, "What do you dare to share?" And again, the best answer is, "What does she want to know?" And what is your intention behind the sharing? If it is just to ease your conscience, you may want to rethink it. Also, how old is she? Someone eighteen versus thirty-something probably has different maturity levels, although a daughter who becomes a mom at an early age may have more maturity or a different perspective on life than one who waits until her mid to late thirties. Then again, someone who still lives at home versus someone who's ventured out on her own will also have different thresholds for information. These contrasts can go on and on. Also, have you been someone who has purged along the way or are you just now seeing some benefit to opening up more, whereas historically you've been more of a closed book?

Yet another example, Alexa, mother of twenty-year-old Tianna, randomly decided to tell her daughter about all of the horrible things Tianna's dad had done to her over the years to explain why they ended up in divorce court when Tianna was sixteen. Not that Tianna hadn't seen with her own eyes her father's bad temper and disregard for her mother, but she really didn't need to get the unedited tabloid news.

As noted, children do observe their parents' behavior and your daughter was likely watching pretty much every move you made.

She had expectations of you and a picture in her mind of what a mother should be. No doubt, you, I, (and the rest of the moms out there) fell short of that ideal image. So rather than hide behind an image, give your daughter some greater clarity and realism of your experience being her mom. I personally think that sharing the context of your life will have great healing benefits as long as it's not used as a blanket hall pass for the mistakes you made along the way. Now for a little assessment of your mother—daughter relationship in particular.

Sugar and Spice Exercise:

When you have some quiet time and space to self-reflect, write out all the things you'd like to share with your daughter to illuminate your core essence. This is a free-flow exercise with no boundaries. Include your experiences and the emotional impact these experiences had on you. This is NOT what you will ultimately share with your daughter. Then pause and go through each item and ask yourself the following questions:

1. How much does she want to know?
2. Why does she want to know?
3. What are the potential consequences if you share some secrets (e.g., will harm result)?
4. Are you just purging your own conscience and you'd be better off (as would she) if you shared it with a friend or therapist instead?
5. How mature is your daughter?
6. Is this what I would have wanted from my own mother? If so, am I just projecting or is my daughter like me and would want this information as well?

7. What's going on in her life right now?
8. Once you've done this thorough assessment, take it one step further. Ask a trusted confidant what they think about the value of sharing. Talk it out and then decide what parts of your diary to express to your adult daughter.

Once you decide what to share with your gal, set aside ample time with her for disclosing and processing the information. Be sensitive to stamina so as not to overwhelm either one of you. Check in with your daughter often as you disclose, encouraging her to be her own spokesperson for when she wants more and when enough is enough. And then be sure to honor her boundaries as well as your own.

CHAPTER 10

"But I Thought You Would": Developing Realistic Expectations for Change

Before embarking on this chapter, please once again acknowledge to yourself that you have come a long way. Maybe you have been implementing some, or all, of the exercises and practices along the way while reading each chapter. Or maybe you've been turning the pages with a broader overview of the tapestry of the relationship you and your daughter have woven. Regardless, you have absorbed a lot and deserve recognition for your open-mindedness and willingness to look more deeply at yourself, both from the point of view of being a daughter and that of being a mother.

As noted, it's far easier to focus our attention on what someone else is doing wrong, or how they are hurting us intentionally or unintentionally, than to turn our attention to our own behavior. However, in the long run it's far better for our overall emotional wellbeing to absorb our own responsibility and accountability for our actions, and the impact they've had on others. You have been willing to do just that by looking in the mirror and trying to understand ways in which you have created or added to the unfulfilling dynamic with your adult daughter. Maybe you'll have even made some progress on the road to communicating more deeply about these things with your daughter, hopefully having received positive feedback or encouragement. Regardless, kudos to you for all your efforts. Many daughters never get the chance to be invited on a healing journey with their mothers, especially from mothers who are willing to be accountable for their own role in their daughters' wounded hearts. Your daughter is lucky to have a mother like you!

Now let's look at some expectations.

Expectations: Reasonable versus Unreasonable

Let's face it, whether we want to or not, we all succumb to creating expectations both of ourselves and of others as this is innate to our human process. No doubt you've had expectations of your daughter in the past as well as presently. And, with such high-intensity processing of information may come even more expectations, like receiving things in return from your dear girl.

While we cannot escape the process of expecting things from life and our experiences within it, we must be particularly mindful of how we act on our expectations and whether they are reasonable (i.e., realistic and spoken, and with agreement from the other), or whether they are unreasonable (i.e., unconscious or unspoken, and without agreement from the other). Granted, this is a common by-product of doing the hard work of raising a daughter and then even more hard work in this healing journey. However, continuing forward with expectations will likely yield more disappointment and heartache. Also, now that you more deeply understand you have no control over anyone else's actions or responses once someone is an independent adult, you can see that creating expectations of your adult daughter may backfire. As a reminder, you may certainly still have influence over your daughter, especially if she has not yet written you off completely or she is still financially dependent on you. However, *she* is ultimately the one in charge of her own actions, reactions, and decision-making process and *you* are only in control of yourself. Hence, our expectations of others, particularly of our daughters, must be kept in check.

Understanding Unreasonable Expectations and Their Consequences:

There's a saying which I believe came out of twelve-step programs (i.e., set of guidelines outlining the course of action for those in recovery who struggle with addictions) that really resonated with me regarding the potential dangers of unchecked expectations. It goes like this: "Expectations are resentments under construction and resentments are like swallowing poison and waiting for the other guy to die." Take a moment and let that really settle in. It's a doozy and rings so true. While that's a very dramatic definition, the reality is that expectations, especially when left unchecked, can wreak havoc on our relationships.

Meet Akari, a fifty-six-year-old mother of three of Japanese descent. Akari enjoyed a super close relationship with her daughter, Hana, until Hana began expressing a desire to flee the nest when she was in her early twenties. Hana had been attending a junior college and lived at home to save money while working at part-time jobs. Her friends were going to get a place together near a job opportunity and she was on board. However, being from a more traditional family wherein the expectation of women was to remain at home until marriage, her mother and father were mortified at the thought of their "innocent" young lady moving out alone into the world. Akari had never even considered that her daughter would desire such independence. Akari had essentially established an unspoken contract with Hana that she would remain at home until marriage to a man. By the way, this also presumed an expectation that Hana would even want to get married, or that she was heterosexual.

Hana was never consulted about this contract. Having been raised in a less-traditional Asian community, Hana did not hold the same values as her folks in this area and she also presumed that her parents, having moved to the States, would have also progressed in their views. Regardless, Hana would never have signed on to this contract had she been consulted about it. Plus, her brothers were encouraged to have their independence. "So why can't I?", she begged. She had no idea that in this modern day she would be held to what she perceived to be a very old, archaic gender stereotype.

Akari had basically mapped out Hana's future without even checking in with her. "After all, this is what my parents did for me and my life turned out just fine," she thought. Hana was not asking for financial support, so Akari actually had very little leverage in this department.

The rift between mother and daughter ensued for a few months as this was no easy challenge for either one of them. They both felt very strongly that the other should comply with her wishes. After several therapy sessions together, mom softened her stance, realizing she was imposing an unrealistic expectation of compliance from her daughter and Hana was able to develop more empathy for her mother's sense of having failed at raising her daughter. Eventually, they were able to have much more adult-to-adult conversations and create conscious, spoken, behavioral contracts to put them both at greater ease. Hana did move out and they engaged in weekly video chats and text messages. Hana agreed she would let her mom know if she were participating in anything out of the ordinary, like going away for a week outside of the country, etc.

In contrast to Akira and Hana's situation, meet Annabel, a thirty-nine-year-old mother of Janelle, who is now twenty. Annabel, who had become a mother at the young age of nineteen, had left home when she was eighteen. She'd fallen in love with her high school sweetheart and contrary to both her and his parent's advice, she and her boyfriend got a place together, barely making ends meet working as grocery store clerks. One night the condom broke. And, well, you know the story. They opted to keep the baby, but the father bailed when Janelle was only a year and a half. Annabel's life became about pure survival and taking care of herself and her baby. Fortunately, her parents didn't turn their backs on her, and they did provide some financial and childcare assistance to their daughter and granddaughter.

For Annabel, while she loved her daughter dearly, she often felt she'd missed out on many of the fun life experiences she observed her friends having. Sometimes she grew resentful and would take it out on Janelle by being snippy and irritable. When Annabel would get an occasional reprieve from work and childcare, she would get annoyed with Janelle for fussing about leaving her behind. "Doesn't my kid know I need some sort of life, too," she'd say in her head. Janelle, in her sweet little girl voice would say, "Mommy, please don't leave me." Then, when mommy left, Janelle would sob uncontrollably in the hands of a barely old enough to babysit pre-teen hired last minute from around the corner.

As Janelle grew up, Annabel sometimes dreamt of the day her daughter would turn eighteen and want to leave home so Annabel could claim some of her youth and lost time by having fun. But to Annabel's surprise, Janelle was in no such hurry. She liked the cozy comfort of hanging out with her mom and figuring things out slowly. Annabel grew increasingly impatient, almost to the point of packing her daughter up and shipping her off somewhere to find her own way.

Annabel had figured all along that her daughter would want to move out to experience the freedom Annabel was never afforded. But unlike the ways in which her parents behaved toward her (i.e., with criticism and judgment), Annabel was prepared to support Janelle's freedom so that she would stave off the type of rebellion Annabel had asserted and have fun as a young, single woman exploring the world. She never imagined that Janelle wouldn't have the hunger she had for a taste of independence.

Annabel had never really spoken to Janelle about these behavioral contracts she had conjured up for her daughter. Rather, she had made assumptions in her own head, expecting that Janelle would follow the road map she'd had all planned out. Janelle, however, had no such plans. As resentments grew, Janelle's sassy factor shot up, too.

Thankfully, once mom and daughter were finally able to sit down and really process things out, addressing both of their needs and expectations, they came up with new agreements. For example, in previous generations children often needed to remain living with their parents or extended family even whilst pursuing their own adulthood goals and dreams. Not because they were being slackers, but rather, because many experienced economic hardships, preventing independent living. Annabel was somewhat of an anomaly to have moved out at such a young age and she hadn't really considered that Janelle had a very different temperament and was more fearful than Annabel had been. Ultimately, they were able to address their differences and together decided on a two-year plan for Janelle to figure out her future goals, including independent living.

These are just two examples of the many ways in which a mom's expectations of her daughter, without her daughter's consent, can backfire. And many of these expectations can become resentments. Once resentment brews it becomes a lot harder to remedy the dynamic. For instance, Akari expected Hana to remain home until marriage. Her intentions weren't to thwart Hana's life. Rather, she believed she was just passing along her generational norm. Yet for Hana, a daughter raised in Western culture with a high regard for independence for all genders, carrying forward this expectation of tradition felt like a jail sentence to a young woman seeking freedom, personal growth, and novel experiences.

Now fast forward to how this relates to you and your healing process with your daughter. As noted, you have taken on quite the journey to tackle building a better bond than what you currently experience with your adult daughter. But she has not necessarily signed up for the same program. So, while you may be excited to get this party started with her, she may need more time to get on board. She may need time to build trust in this process by experiencing your sincerity in coming to this from a new and better perspective and approach. Also, she may be harboring her own resentments from unmet expectations she created through her own unconscious process or unchecked entitlement. Basically, these unspoken behavioral contracts can go both ways, but all you can do is work on your own. Hopefully, by doing so, you pave the way for your daughter to look at hers so that you can both create new conscious behavioral contracts wherein you both make agreements you can keep, based on realistic and spoken expectations.

Creating Healthy Behavioral Contracts

We've all been in some sort of situation wherein we have had to sign a contract and agree to the terms set out in said document. The contract delivers all the information necessary for you to decide whether to proceed or not. In essence you've been provided with informed consent. In legal matters, attorneys spend hours upon hours, possibly on your dime, making sure the contract is enforceable and that both parties are ultimately protected. Maybe you've purchased a car recently, signed a lease, or opened a line of credit. If so, then you know you're required to fulfil certain obligations and, so too, is the other side. Of course, things can still go badly, especially if someone doesn't respect the terms of the contract. But, in most cases with decent human beings these types of contracts spell out as much as possible, and in the clearest terms, what is precisely expected of each person.

We have other types of contracts, like the plans you make for lunch with a friend. You both agree on a place and a time and unless there are extenuating circumstances you probably end the conversation with both of you having clarity on the terms. Maybe other details get ironed out once at the restaurant, like whether you're going to split the check, or if one of you is treating the other. But in the end, you're both clear on where to meet and when.

Then there are even softer contracts, like asking your intimate partner to take out the garbage cans after work. Your partner agrees, but no definitive time has been agreed upon. To you "after work" may mean "right away after work" whereas your partner may interpret that to mean anytime from getting home to going to bed or even doing it the next morning. After all, the garbage service might not be showing up for a few days. As you can see, these softer contracts can become messier and leave more room for disappointments based on unmet expectations.

But the absolute messiest and potentially dangerous contracts of all are the unconscious, or even conscious but unspoken, expectations wherein you're holding another person mentally hostage as if the other has signed on the dotted line and has failed to meet a promise never known to him or her. Trust me, everyone on the planet has fallen victim to being the recipient of someone's unconscious behavioral contract and the creator of one.

Sometimes we deny or choose not to share our expectations because we don't feel like we really have a right to have them. Nevertheless, even if we choose not to name them out loud, they still lurk in the background and can lead to developing resentment. So, it's always best to just acknowledge what they are and then see if you can modify them. Healthy behavioral contracts include the following characteristic:

1. They are based on conscious thought.
2. They are realistic to the particular person (your daughter in this case) with whom you're making the contract.
3. They are spoken.
4. They are made by both parties.
5. They include clauses or discussions about when or how an agreement can be changed.
6. They can be one-sided, if named as such. For example, I can make a promise to my daughter to call her every week and she has every right to hold me to this promise. But she is not obligated to answer or even return my call if that's not part of the agreement. Sometimes we make these types of agreements to hold ourselves accountable through another person's eyes.

This description may sound rather mechanical and lawyerly. And this may be so, but the creation of these contracts is really just about owning your expectations, seeing whether they are worth pursuing through agreement with your daughter, giving her the details, and allowing her to accept or decline the terms. All of this is in service of minimizing disappointment and resentment.

Now, let's put an end to unconscious behavioral contracts based on unrealistic expectations by finishing off with a little sugar and spice exercise.

Sugar and Spice Exercise: Identifying Your Expectations and Removing Resentments

Name five things you have expected from your daughter (e.g., that she would earn a college degree, she would be straight and marry a guy, she would provide you with grandchildren, etc.). You can certainly name more but try to stick to the major ones to not overwhelm yourself. Again, this is a process of self-exploration and learning, not self-loathing, guilt-promoting, or shame-inducing. Also, when making your list, please distinguish those things you wish or hope for your daughter (e.g., that she will experience happiness and joy) from what you expected of her (e.g., that she will call you whenever something significant happens in her life). Next, distinguish each item on your list as to whether they are reasonable (something she agreed to) versus unreasonable (your own unspoken expectation with no agreement).

Once you've separated out the two different types of expectations, consider writing your daughter a letter letting her know that you have become aware of certain expectations you made of her and that you now realize these were unfair since she was not part of creating an agreement. Make note of any disappointment or resentment you held regarding her lack of meeting your expectations, heavily emphasizing your own acknowledgement of responsibility. Then ask her for her forgiveness and understanding.

Consider those items where you believe you did have a mutual agreement and she did not follow through on her end. For instance, she said she'd invite you over for dinner in the next few weeks and now it's been two months. Or she's offered to help you clean out your garage of her old stuff and every time you try to get her to commit to a time, she avoids you. Include in the letter that you'd love the opportunity to understand more deeply what was going on for her that caused her to break her agreement with you. Be careful not to sound accusatory. Rather, practice gentleness to really try to get a sense of why she would make agreements and not keep them. Did she make agreements out of fear or pressure from you, not believing she had permission to decline? Or maybe she thought she wanted to do whatever she promised, but then had a change of heart and didn't know how to tell you directly, attempting to avoid you feeling disappointed in her?

You can decide whether you want to focus this exploration on recent times, confined to her as an adult. Or you may want to dive further, if she's available, into understanding her perspective from her childhood memories.

If you choose not to write this letter to send to your daughter, at the very least, please write it for yourself, vowing to become as conscious as possible regarding your expectations of yourself and of your daughter for the future. Then write yourself a forgiveness letter. Even thinking about mastering the art of creating reasonable expectations of yourself and others is a huge step toward having a more peaceful and joyful life. And when those disappointments inevitably arise, you'll have a much better opportunity to note them, see your part, and leave the resentment train behind you

CHAPTER 11

Failure to Launch or Re-launch

In contemporary Western society, particularly in metropolitan areas, it has often been the norm, and even expected, that when your daughter reaches a certain age (or level of maturity) she'll flee the nest and create a life of her own. And since the desire to spread our wings and fly is as natural to the developmental process as is a dog yearning to sniff another dog's butt while walking in the neighborhood, it's almost a mother's job to encourage her daughter to take the leap. In our culture, we even define adulthood as beginning as young as eighteen years old. (Though we may have to reconsider this whole concept since findings from neuroscience show that the brain isn't even fully developed until one's mid-twenties.) But that's a topic for another book. Suffice it to say that the desire for her identity search away from you is a natural and healthy process.

Often, this launching process occurs as result of choosing to move away to go to college or just simply because she wants her independence. She may want to move in with a lover or a platonic friend. She'll become determined to explore her own identity, no longer specifically in relation to her mother and other caregivers, but rather, in relation to herself. This is not because of lack of love for her family, but rather, because of a natural urge to separate and individuate.

It may be time for her to earn her own money. Her parents may have even been kicked out of their own homes in their young adulthood and told it's time to make their own way in the world. "We have done our job, now it's time for you to do yours!", some have heard and shared with their own kids. In many subcultures, girls are more coddled and may be less likely to actually make the move, but the developmental journey presses all of us at some point to pursue our independence. And as parents, we generally want our children to thrive on their own despite having some of our own fears of an empty nest syndrome.

Speaking of empty nest syndrome, I'll never forget the time when my daughter, Tiffany, went off to college. After getting her settled in her dorm and returning home, I opened the refrigerator door and was drawn to some leftover items specific to her food preferences. Out of nowhere, I burst into tears! It had nothing to do with the food, of course. The realization that she would rarely be at the dinner table now just hit me like a ton of bricks. Sure, I had psychologically prepared for what I presumed would be an inevitable departure. In fact, at times I'd been counting the days for her launch because the tumultuous teens took a toll on both of us. Nevertheless, I had no idea her leaving would cause such a deep emotional sadness in my heart akin to a child's despair when no longer being allowed to have the pacifier. I still wanted to have her close to me and within my mothering den, but it was clear she wasn't coming back to live with me.

For the first week or two, my mind went racing to places like, "I've lost my daughter! Will I even see her again?" I missed her terribly. Granted, once I came back to a more rational, less purely emotional state, I came to accept that as long as life didn't throw us too many curve balls, she and I would see each other on a fairly regular basis. Fast forward, I had no idea that she would decide to travel around the world only to have the COVID-19 pandemic strike, leaving her planted in Egypt for more than a year. Granted, thanks to modern technology, I was still able to have video contact with her so it certainly wasn't as painful of a separation as it could have been.

When I went off to college, only about eighty miles from my home base, my parents didn't actually take me there. Instead, I packed up my car and drove off to meet the new world of college challenges. My situation was a bit different, however, because just before my senior year of high school, my parents had moved out of my childhood home to a new location about twenty-five miles away. There was no way I was going to shift schools after spending the last eleven years with my childhood friend group. (Yup—that was my sassy and rude attitude!) At that point, I'd also been working as a waitress and had developed a group of friends quite a bit older than I was. Many of them let me crash on their couches on school days so I wouldn't have to commute so far to complete high school.

While I was pretty hurt that my parents weren't more engaged in my official launch, after a while I had a different perspective. I guess for my folks, it wasn't that big of a transition for me to go off to college since I hadn't spent much time at home the prior year. Plus, of even greater relevance, my parents had both been largely on their own from very early ages in comparison to our norm. My mother, for instance, left her own abusive family system in her teens and was fully self-supporting by the time she was eighteen without even a high school diploma, so that was their point of reference. In hindsight, I think my mom was pretty sad when I left home, though she never shared these feelings. I, of course, wanted my daughter to have a more "loving" experience of venturing out into the world outside her home.

By the way, I'm not looking for sympathy here. Neither my experience with my own parents, nor my experience with Tiffany with regards to launching is a sob story. We fared better than most during her fleeing of the nest and also during the pandemic. I know many moms who've lost their daughters to drug addiction, running off with an abusive lover and becoming missing in action, or even ultimately getting the worst news ever of her daughter's death. I can only hope your stories are more like mine and not the latter. Nevertheless, the launching process can be challenging to both mother and daughter, but ultimately, it's a healthy step in one's development.

In today's world of economic volatility, and especially with the COVID-19 pandemic, this whole launching thing has become more complicated. Hordes of young women have needed to stay hunkered down at home or return to home due to financial hardship, loss of job, divorce, or needing help with their own young child. Many women developed mental health issues such as depression or anxiety because of repercussions from the pandemic. Not to mention dealing with actual illness and its fallout, such as long COVID syndrome.

Any or all of these factors above can have a significant effect on the separation/individuation process. So, if your adult daughter has not yet left the nest or needed to return for various reasons, this next section may help you put into greater perspective the struggles between the two of you.

Separation and Individuation

Volumes upon volumes have been written regarding the process of separation and individuation to better understand the course of human development. While it began as a theory centered upon early childhood development by psychoanalyst Margaret Mahler, back in 1950, it has many applications in adulthood as well. And, while I'm certain more and more will be revealed over time as the research becomes more sophisticated in truly understanding the course of human development, what we understand thus far remains relevant here. So, let's take a small detour into understanding the concept of the separation and individuation process and how that may be playing a role in your daughter's sassiness.

Remember when your daughter resided in your womb? You and she were one with each other. Completely symbiotic. She relied exclusively on you for her survival. And then, birth happens and this little being is left on her own to breathe. Talk about a rude transition!

Once we are born, we become disengaged from our mother's life force. Yep, as soon as the cord is cut, we are at the mercy of our own lungs, among other things. Separation has begun. In previous generations, it was standard practice to take the baby away from the mother. Fortunately, thanks to our growing understanding of the importance of those first few moments regarding bonding, most birthing experiences have become gentler and more attuned to attachment, though we still have a long way to go. Nevertheless, it is at that moment of birth that the newborn begins the journey of separation and individuation, ultimately to be able to thrive in the world independently.

Naturally, your daughter didn't only need you while in the womb. She also needed you for quite some time to care for her myriad and complex needs, but the two of you were no longer attached physically. And slowly but surely, she also began to see her own image as being different from yours; that is, as individuated. Even if you are an adoptive mom, the developmental process still requires her to become her own person psychologically. A loving and secure emotional attachment to her caregiver facilitates a smoother process.

As you can see this can be a very delicate balance as life will often derail our best intentions to stay attuned to our children. All kinds of things can derail a child from developing a secure attachment and thereby complicate the separation/individuation process. Some of the many life events having potential consequences include: a parental divorce, a move due to relocation for a new job, mental illness, and the death of a loved one. The list goes on and on. The good news is that children are very resilient—they can weather a lot of ups and downs. But, no doubt, these events and how they were processed (or not processed) may have left some emotional wounds in both mother and daughter that are worthy of healing.

So, it's quite possible that some of the conflicts you face with your gal may have to do with disruptions in the separation and individuation process and she's struggling to find her own identity. Sometimes we can also find more empathy when we look back at our own struggles with our moms in reference to this process.

Leslie, a highly independent sixty-three-year-old divorcee, set out to enjoy the world through travel, biking, and hiking. Her daughter, Virginia, age twenty-eight, hadn't set out to live on her own primarily due to financial limitations. And, quite frankly, the accommodations at home were posh. On the surface, these two women seemed to enjoy a fairly healthy relationship and living arrangement. However, they began arguing more severely once Virginia started making more noise about actually moving out with some friends. Leslie, of course, wanted her daughter to shine on her own. But unconsciously, she "needed" her daughter to stay with her because she was quite lonely and had been unknowingly relying on her daughter to be her companion to fill up her empty heart. Mind you, no one would have guessed this to be the case given how much Leslie was out and about on her adventures.

Leslie and her ex-husband divorced when Virginia was about fifteen. Virginia wasn't really close to her dad, so she wasn't that bent out of shape about it. She saw him on occasion but mostly lived with her mom. Her mom was heavily involved in Virginia's sports and academics and Virginia didn't really mind. She was more of a homebody herself and enjoyed the company of just a few select friends. She didn't date much and struggled with trying to figure out what to do with her future. She dabbled in some different jobs but hadn't really found her niche. Leslie didn't date much either, and the two of them were more like sisters than mother and daughter.

While their relationship usually flowed smoothly with only a few glitches, once Virginia was about twenty-five-years-old she found her way into a career in private coaching. Within a few years, she was able to save enough to make the big move to her own place, feeling confident in her ability to support herself. Unfortunately, Leslie and Virginia got entangled in a co-dependent mess. Leslie hadn't realized how much she "needed" her daughter to be around and would say and do things to chip away at Virginia's confidence. And Virginia, who had sort of become her mom's confidant and security blanket, didn't want to abandon her mom, but she also wanted her own space. It became a miserable power struggle for both. Fortunately, with help, aiding in greater self-reflection and awareness, they were able to disentangle themselves from one another and build a healthier relationship based on mutual admiration and respect. Leslie needed to build adult relationships with others to fulfill her loneliness.

Sugar and Spice Exercise:

Now it's time for you to try another exercise in self-reflection. Can you think of ways in which the separation and individuation process may have been thwarted along the way? Below are some questions to guide you. Please do not address these with self-loathing or shame. We've all disturbed the delicate balance of healthy separation and individuation in one way or another. Remember, the entire purpose of this book is to help you become better equipped to understand and empathize with your daughter's internal experience of her development, heal the leftover wounds (both within you and within her), and bring back some sugar and spice.

Please review the questions below and answer as best as your memory allows. It may also be valuable to address these questions from the perspective of your own separation and individuation process from your mother and whether you may have also carried any leftovers into your adulthood and in your motherhood role. Be careful not to rush this process.

1. Were there any significant losses? (Possibly a divorce, a move, or a new job that took more of your time away from your daughter?)
2. Did your daughter witness high levels of conflict without healthy resolution, either between you and someone else in the household or among other members in the family?
3. Was there any abuse such as sexual, psychological, emotional, or physical?
4. Was chemical dependency an issue your daughter witnessed in someone in the family?
5. Did or does your daughter suffer from addiction of any sort? (Drugs, alcohol, eating disorder, gambling, debt, gaming, etc.)
6. Did your daughter witness mental health issues in the family? (Nuclear or closely extended)
7. Did or does your daughter suffer from mental health issues?
8. Do you and your daughter have a co-dependent relationship where you have fostered her to stay dependent on you for your sense of self-value?
9. Does your daughter's independence (or desire for such) threaten you in any way?

10. Were you overly protective or overly permissive?
11. Are there any other relevant events in your daughter's life that may have influenced the healthiness of her ability to separate and individuate?

Make note of your answers, understanding that they may not come to you right away. You may find that I didn't ask the right questions for you, so please ask yourself those you perceive to be more relevant.

If you become inclined, you can share this exercise with your daughter, letting her know what you discovered about yourself. And then invite her to share more deeply her own experience around finding her identity and what you may be able to do now to encourage the process for her. It may still serve her well to continue living at home, but at least you will create a healthier environment for all to thrive because you will now have conscious and open communication, and boundaries fitting to the living situation.

Eventually, you'll also need to start a dialogue with your daughter concerning a specific plan around her moving out, addressing when she will leave, what she'll need to make that happen, where she will go, etc. You may both decide that she can stay indefinitely but only with established respectful boundaries.

Please note that even if your daughter has left the nest and hasn't returned, there may still be issues around her sense of being able to be separate and individuate. For example, she may perceive you as too clingy and fear that if she finds her way without your help that you will experience unbearable separation anxiety. Or she may lack confidence in herself and feel like she needs to hold onto you as her guidance counselor. So, for whatever reason she still struggles despite living outside of your home, the nuances of her separation and individuation process are still a valuable conversation to have with yourself and with her.

CHAPTER 12

Setting Limits Lovingly

Moms who are at times plagued with guilt, shame, or fear may have difficulty saying no to their children, particularly to their daughters. Have you ever felt this way? Also, if you felt wounded by your mom in whatever way, you probably walked a tightrope in an attempt to prevent emotional hurt in your daughter—and you're not a circus performer! You wanted to give her the moon, often erring on the side of being "too nice." And as you learned in Chapter Five, "The Too Nice Moms Club", you may have been overly zealous, smothering her with yeses, unearned allowances for chores she never finished, boundless adventures, and freedoms. (Possibly even those inappropriate to her developmental age, etc.). You meant no harm. You wanted to shower her with love and keep her from experiencing any pain. But no matter how hard you tried, some cracks occurred, and she suffered anyway in her own ways. No mom can do it all or prevent the inevitable growing pains we all endure.

This description by no means implies that you were an inadequate mother in any way. Remember, that would be a "shame" word and that's the last state of being I would ever want for you. You know you tried your best. Like many moms, you may have read books on how to raise a healthy child and you diligently tried to adjust your ways to please her. Inadvertently, however, in her mind something was either not enough or too much. No perfect score exists, and if you thought there could be, you were doomed from the get-go. For our purposes you're a winner and you'll stay as such as long as you continue trying your best, even if your daughter can't appreciate you at this time. My point in saying all this is just to let you know even if you made some pretty big mistakes, as we all have, that doesn't deny you the right to remain self-caring and to set limits. (Lovingly, of course.)

What we need to be careful of is to not do too much of a 180-degree turnaround. Just like training a puppy can be a slow and arduous process, the repair work with your daughter may take a lot of time and energy, requiring lots of patience and tender loving care both for yourself and for your daughter. Plus, these limits, also known as boundaries, may not initially be very well received. Your daughter may have developed quite a sense of entitlement and expectation that it is your job for the rest of your life to make up for whatever she felt did not work well for her. She may not even know this consciously. But her actions may speak of demandingness and her self-righteousness may fire up when you start saying no. She may even act punitively toward you and then accuse you of withholding your love from her. While the idea of being the recipient of an even more sassy and rude attitude from her may worry or scare you, for any relationship to thrive healthy boundaries need to be set.

I wish an exact roadmap existed on how to set healthy boundaries but, in reality, the process is much more of an art, beginning with a slab of clay being morphed along the way. So, let's start learning by example.

Keisha, a thirty-four-year-old biotech specialist, felt her mom favored her brother over her. Her mom, Lavender, would be the first to admit that she spent more time with her son, Slade, because both she and Slade shared a love for athletics whereas Keisha was much more of a brainy child. While Lavender often praised Keisha for her high academic achievements, Keisha always felt that her mom's heart was rooted much more heavily into her brother.

During her teens, Keisha became quite demanding of her mother's attention and anytime her mother was unable to meet her demands, Keisha would verbally attack her or withdraw and remain distant from the family. Lavender, of course, did not love her son any more than she loved her daughter. She just felt she had more similarities to Slade's interests. In fact, in some ways Lavender felt inadequate in relation to her daughter's intelligence and didn't know how to relate to her as easily as she could with her son.

While Keisha's verbal attacks dwindled to some degree when she entered adulthood and went off to college, her expectations that her mother would spend a lifetime compensating for favoring her brother did not and her demandingness of her mother continued to climb. Lavender simply did not know how to remedy this tragic situation and she grew more and more resentful toward her daughter and, not so surprisingly, she did start to favor her son.

Lavender needed to learn that it was okay for her to set boundaries. At first, she was quite defensive and a bit like lightning hitting a telephone pole, adding fuel to the fire and giving Keisha even more license to berate her and demand more from her. By the time they came to my office, they were in pretty dire straits. Thankfully, after multiple rounds of Lavender acknowledging Keisha's emotional hurt without defending herself, Keisha's pain and protective shield began to dissipate. While Lavender didn't agree with Keisha's perception that she loved Slade any more than her, she learned she needed to honor that this was what Keisha experienced and hold space for it. Later, they both came to appreciate that as adults still intertwined in each other's lives, Lavender should not be expected to spend her life making up for Keisha's childhood wounds. Keisha needed to find forgiveness in her heart and come to realize that what a child believes is what's so is not always what's so. Yet her experience still needed to be validated. During this healing process they both learned the importance of establishing and maintaining boundaries. This did not come easily to them, but, with practice, the process became smoother, with neither of them feeling insulted.

You, too, can find your own gentle voice to set limits with love to continue your healing journey for yourself and for your relationship with your daughter.

Guidelines for Healthy Boundaries and Limits

If you recall, in the previous chapter on failure to launch, I described the separation and individuation process of development. That concept and process applies to understanding the concept of boundaries, as well. When a child becomes physically separated from the mother, once leaving the womb, this establishes the beginnings of physical boundaries. As the child individuates, she also establishes new psychological and emotional boundaries. Both move along a continuum with the process continuing and fluctuating throughout the lifespan. We all have boundaries, both physical and psychological, but how we assert these boundaries varies across individuals and within any given relationship. The health and wellness of our boundaries can be affected by many different variables including the quality and nature of a relationship and interaction, age, level of dependency on another, our relationship and trust in our own selves, etc.

Of course, taking all these factors into play and creating an example of each would be far too complex. Nevertheless, a few highlights seem quite important as they relate to the relationship between you and your daughter.

Physical boundaries: A physical boundary is exactly what it sounds like. It's the boundary that allows us to put physical space between ourselves and another. If you ever used the time-out or time-in method of discipline with your daughter, you were creating a physical boundary between the two of you. Or, if you went out for date night, you also created physical space between the two of you. When children are young, they don't have much control over their physical boundaries and the ability to regulate how much space they need. They're pretty much at the mercy of what their caregivers allow. Many parents, yourself maybe included, push their kids to give hugs to those whom the parents believe the child should be showing affection. "Go give your Uncle John a hug," you might request. Most of the time, these situations are harmless. But you can see that if the child doesn't want to give the hug, she may not feel like she has much choice.

Once a child gets older, however, she usually has much more authority as to where and with whom she shares her physical space. Ideally, she also gets full choice as to how or by whom her body gets touched. When we feel safe and willing to be vulnerable, we may have the need for closer contact with one another. Conversely, when we are frightened or angry with someone or with whom we lack trust, we may want to erect very strict physical boundary as if to say, "Stay the fuck away from me." No doubt, you and your daughter experienced the full array of physical boundaries from snuggles and cuddles (lowest level of boundary) to, "Mom, get out of my room!" (high level of physical boundary).

Sometimes physical boundaries are not necessarily what's desired but what makes the most sense given a particular context. For instance, you may want your daughter to live close by, but she chose a college several thousand miles away to accommodate her major and facilitate the best chance for her career success. Or the reverse, you may have wanted much greater space between you and your daughter, but it made the most sense to keep her close by. Maybe it was more financially prudent. Most of these accommodations are mindless and relatively painless when two people get along well. But creating healthy physical space can become quite a bit more challenging if the relationship is already strained.

Psychological and emotional boundaries: Equally as important, though not as readily observable, is the development of psychological boundaries—i.e., those internal edges that regulate how close we allow someone to come into our emotional and mental space. With a psychological boundary, we can be in the same room together, but we may feel as if we might as well be across the planet from one another without any means of communication. This is a rigid boundary of shutting someone out. Conversely, we could be across the world from one another and still be emotionally bonded.

Again, when a child is young, she has not yet individuated enough to know her own psychological separateness. But boy, once those toddler years kick in, you can see right before your eyes the push for your little one to assert her own self. The word NO becomes a dominant force in the household.

As we develop and mature, our psychological boundaries are reflected by the statement that, "Whether we are far apart physically, or even in very close proximity to one another, I'm still my own person, able to have my own thoughts, feelings, and reactions separate from yours." There is no need to rebel because there is an internal, grounded knowing that this is what's so. We can feel close to someone because of trust and respect and still honor our differences.

When our ability to create healthy psychological and/or physical boundaries gets thwarted or goes awry, messiness ensues. Then we often see relationships that are co-dependent in nature with a constant need for validation and approval from another, persistent power struggles, fear of abandonment, lack of motivation, inability to self-regulate, or just overall stress and distress.

Many of us struggle throughout our lifespan learning how to overcome our own disruptions in healthy boundary setting so it's no wonder this would also play out in our relationship with our daughters. But don't despair. All the contents in this book thus far have been aimed at facilitating this process. Now, for some specific guidance in creating healthy boundaries with your adult daughter.

Ingredients for Healthy Boundaries

We need many ingredients to create healthy boundaries with our grown daughters. Mind you, if you're at all still caught up in your own sense of victimhood, these items may not be easy to come by. But, by doing your best, you will be able to yield a tempting feast. And even if your daughter still refuses to dine with you, you'll know you put out quite the spread!

1. *Be respectful of the limits set by either of you.* You can ask for modifications or clarifications but be careful not to become a boundary violator. For instance, if your daughter asks you to give her space in this process, honor her request but ask for specifics as to what that means to her. Or, if you tell your daughter you're no longer going to pay her way for something, don't cave in if she tries to manipulate you. You can always change your own boundary—but do so consciously and intentionally, not under pressure or duress.

2. *Honor yourself and your own needs.* You matter, too, in this process and throughout the rest of your life. So don't forget about yourself!

3. *Be kind and loving.* I've emphasized this throughout the book because it's so essential. You don't need angry, unnecessary outbursts, no matter how wronged you may feel. Instead, stay centered in your love for her, knowing that you, too, can create your own necessary psychological and physical boundaries.

4. *Start with the assumption that your daughter loves you, despite her actions.* Unless she has told you otherwise, she's hurt and apprehensive, maybe doubting whether things can change for the better between the two of you. But that doesn't mean she no longer cares deeply for you. Trust she's also doing the best she can with the tools she has available.

5. *It's okay to say "NO!"* If necessary, you may need to set very strong impermeable boundaries, but be cautious not to retaliate. Be centered and thoughtful when you choose to be extra firm.

6. *Make "I" statements whenever possible.* It's often tempting to point the finger and say something like, "I'm doing this because *you*..." But that's not really an "I" statement. Rather, it's a "you" statement in disguise. Instead, try, "I'm setting this limit because *I*..."

7. *You are the expert only for your own self and your own needs.* And the same goes for your daughter. She is the expert concerning herself. So, listen to what she says and listen to yourself. You shouldn't have to be a mind reader or second-guess everything she says or does. She's an adult now and needs to learn to communicate clearly.

8. *Be genuine and sincere.* When we can be authentic, we have the best chance of touching someone else's heart.

9. *Be flexible.* Being flexible doesn't have to equate with wishy-washiness. Healthy boundaries have an ebb and flow. Whereas at this point you may need certain boundaries in a more rigid fashion, as things progress, we can become softer and more fluid with the edges we set around us. So just like you may need to bundle up with gloves, a scarf, and a thick down jacket when you're heading out into a snowstorm, you wouldn't want to wear this same gear when walking on a warm sandy beach in the Bahamas.

To illuminate, see the example below of a letter written by a mom, crafted together with me, to her daughter Megan, a twenty-year-old exploratory adventurer, after having a very strained conversation regarding an upcoming holiday visit.

Sample Boundary Letter:

Dearest Megan,

I'm sad that we are once again not in a great place with each other. I hate it when you're unhappy and I think you don't like it when I'm upset, especially when it has to do with you. I'd like to try to help us get through this unpleasant situation by communicating better. Here's my take on things:

Up until last week, I was under the impression that you were not coming home for the holidays. Although I was sad about that, I took the opportunity to plan a "real" trip for myself. Not just a weekend getaway, or a "pseudo-trip" like those getaways that were wrapped around helping you find colleges, moving you to college, helping you set up your apartment, etc., but an actual vacation. Once I had my trip planned, I was looking forward to it immensely. I assumed you were happy with your decision not to come home, and I made the best of it.

Last night, during our conversation, you let me know that you'd changed your plans and are now coming home *and* with a boyfriend whom I had not yet met. I was a little bummed because, given my vacation plans, I wasn't going to get to see you. But I was happy that you would be able to see your friends and spend time at your dad's house. When we hung up, I thought we were both cool. During our chat you never mentioned anything about expecting to use my car or my house so I operated from our understanding that you're independent and can take care of yourself. After all, you've been telling me for months that you're happy figuring things out about your life and the directions you have been taking. And I'm working very hard to come to acceptance and appreciation of your current life path.

Surprisingly, later that night, I woke up with a huge sense of anxiety and I spent two to three hours awake, not being able to figure out why I was so nervous. Then it dawned on me that you might have expectations of me that you hadn't expressed. Hence, I figured it would be better to nip any potential conflicts we may have in the bud by writing you a letter stating my "comfort zone" of boundaries, which included no use of my car, and no staying at my house while I'm away. I had anticipated that you wouldn't be entirely happy about what I stated, but I figured that, given all that I've done for you, you would be appreciative of what I was offering to you during your visit.

When we talked last night, I was quite hurt when you said that "I'll never understand you." (Or words to that effect.) Granted, you admirably attempted to deflect a fight and you never demanded that I change my mind. I really appreciate that!

But it really hurt that your takeaway from all of this was that I don't understand you at all. Gosh, I believe that I've gone above and beyond to get to know you and your current values. I've even made several attempts to meet your boyfriend (via Skype, phone, or in-person) but you've declined all offers. Plus, I've continued to be emotionally and financially supportive in every way that I can. Yet I often still get the sense that whatever I do isn't enough, and you want more.

Megan, I love you with all my heart. But I don't want to feel guilty for setting boundaries around my stuff. A pattern I've noticed with us is that we seem to go along just fine as long as all of your needs are met, and I have no expectations of you. You tell me not to worry about things and that all is good. But then when you want something, you tend to wait until the last minute and then expect (often without even communicating what you want or believe you need) that I'll comply and fulfill whatever it is that you desire. Then when I have trepidations, etc., you perceive me as the one who has failed you and I end up feeling bad. This is not a healthy dynamic. I'm trying to take responsibility for my part in this, but I'm not sure that you see your part in it. I need to work on letting go of feeling guilty, especially when I'm certain I've done nothing wrong. I recognize that I sometimes fall into the trap of allowing your actions to make me feel bad and then I get upset with you. I need to take responsibility for my own feelings.

Well, that is enough focus on what happened. Now, on to what I wish would have happened (maybe as a lesson for the future) and a proposal to help remedy this distress between us.

Basically, had you stated your assumptions or asked me questions about what would be possible to make your visit the best it could be, I think we could have avoided this whole upset. I would have found it more thoughtful of you if you had said something like, "Hey, Mom, I'm actually coming down for the holiday. I know I've told you that I really don't care about cars and stuff, but if it's possible can I use the Camry when I'm in town? Also, I'd really like to spend time with my boyfriend, and I know you don't know him. Are you comfortable with my bringing him to the house? I suppose I could stay at my dad's if that's better, but I'd rather stay at your house. Please let me know your thoughts."

Had you at least shown some sensitivity that you were expecting something of me outside of our current agreement, without being presumptuous that I would know your needs, I think this would have gone better. Now I'm in the quandary of not wanting to cave in and altering my boundaries, yet I also want to leave town and not feel this sense of distress because you are not happy.

What I propose is that when you change your plans or want to change agreements, you take responsibility for communicating what your wishes are, without the expectation that I should comply. I really get upset when I feel a sense of entitlement from you and a dismissal of all my ongoing generosity.

Concerning the use of the spare car, I'm willing to allow you to use it. However, I am not comfortable allowing you to have people over whom I've not met and who do not know me. Again, I know that you are a very trusting person, but I can't put my personal property at risk, so I need to err on the side of caution. Hence, please stay with friends or at your dad's house. I'm hoping you'll give all this some deep consideration. I'm open to talking sometime between now and the weekend.

Much love always,

Mom

Meagan initially responded with irritation and defensiveness. But fortunately, because of previous healing work they'd done together, they were able to talk this snag through and come up with an agreement acceptable to both of them.

Sugar and Spice Exercise:

Take a few moments and practice delivering a boundary you've wanted to share with your daughter but have been afraid of the fallout. Try integrating as many, if not all, of the ingredients listed above. Practice writing it out several times and play with different versions. I suggest that on the first try, free write no holds barred, without censorship or modification. You might be angry, resentful, and even in a state where you feel you've been wronged and with a "Why the heck do I need to reach out to her," state of mind. No worries. That's normal. Just make sure you don't accidentally press send on the uncensored version. After you've taken a few stabs at it, put it aside for a day or two and then revisit it, making especially certain that your tone is loving and kind. You don't have to sugar-coat it. But be mindful of what you're saying and how you're saying it. Then read it to a trusted friend or loved one who can give you some feedback on reference points you may have missed. Once you've done all these steps, take the plunge and send it.

Please note: As stated initially in the Introduction, this book is not a step-by-step guide, nor written in a particularly linear fashion. Nevertheless, I do advise, considering you've made some headway with your daughter regarding making amends and building a new foundation together, you'd practice this other step first. But you know your daughter and your situation. I don't. Just give this some thought before you proceed.

CHAPTER 13

Get a Little Help from Your Friends or Intimate Partner

The endeavor of healing a mother—daughter relationship can be a monumental effort and tough to bear alone. While you may see no other options but to fly solo, most of us, even lone wolves, can use a little help now and again. Sometimes we may even need a lot of help. While I certainly hope that the guidance throughout this book has served you something akin to having a life coach by your side, having a trusted friend or intimate partner can also be a welcome added resource.

Mind you, I'm not suggesting that you have someone else step in to do the communicating for you on your behalf. Although the thought of someone else being your mouthpiece may sound good to you, especially if your relationship with your daughter has become highly contentious or she's shunning you, this would not be healthy in the long run. Hence, you'll still need to be front and center in this process. However, there are several ways in which others can be enlisted to make the process more supportive for you. And that may even be someone who steps in to facilitate starting the process.

Let's meet Wendy, a forty-eight-year-old mother, and Sharon, her nineteen-year-old daughter. Sharon, who lives with her boyfriend and two other roommates, has a full-time job as a nanny. Around age sixteen, Sharon's sassy factor began climbing through the roof, becoming increasingly rude toward her mom. From Sharon's point of view, her dad, Peter, was the good one and mom became the pain in the ass. Wendy would often cry out to Peter, "I'm losing our daughter. I feel so sad and hopeless."

Peter, a very practical, non-emotional guy, would give Wendy a quick hug during these moments and tell her to stop making such a big deal out of nothing. This would only make Wendy feel worse. She wanted Peter to fix it, but she knew in her heart she had to find a way to reach Sharon.

Wendy never had a very close relationship with her mom, whom she would describe as cold and distant. Her dad was the warmer of the two and she often wished he would help her mom warm up to her, but he never saw this as his role. While Peter and Wendy's dads were quite different, they also shared a similarity in their hands-off approach to relationships matters.

Eventually, Wendy came to realize that Peter might actually be able to provide some assistance in her efforts to build a closer bond with their daughter. "But how?" she asked. "Well," I said, "let's draft a script, outlining specific ways in which he can help." As our conversation unfolded, we agreed it seemed best if Peter would be willing to have a heart-to-heart chat with Sharon, letting her know that her mom was suffering and truly wanted to have a better relationship with her, and for Sharon to give her mom a chance. Also, since Peter was seen as the good one, he could use his influence to help Sharon see that she had a role in her mother's distress and for her to open up to possibilities of repair. Thankfully, Peter was amenable to these suggestions, and he was instrumental in creating an opening for his wife and daughter to start a new dialogue.

Clearly, these efforts to engage a significant other in the healing process won't always yield a positive outcome. However, maybe it's worth a try. Now, let's look at from whom, when, and how to seek assistance, and define the assistance needed.

Guidance for Seeking Assistance

1. *First and foremost, only seek assistance from someone you truly trust and who you believe won't betray you.* That may seem like such a no-brainer, but I can't tell you how many moms, with their wounded hearts, become desperate and reach out to anyone just to try to get some validation for their agony. Some may even vilify their daughters, yielding pity from others. Or they may choose people who have hidden agendas—i.e., those who receive some benefit from your distress or may even enjoy the drama on some level. While we can never really know whether someone will betray us or not, if we have a long history of loyalty to that person, that's a pretty good gauge.

2. *Seek guidance, advice, and/or assistance from those who can be reasonably unbiased and who can understand both sides.* This could be a friend, relative, or significant other. Regardless, be careful to select someone who is both compassionate and level-headed. Avoid drama queens!

3. *Define what kind of assistance you're seeking.* Do you simply need a shoulder to cry on? Or do you need someone to be a sounding board with whom you can practice what you want to say or write to your daughter? Or would you like someone to help you get your daughter's attention? Remember, no one can

do the work for you, but someone might be able to help start the process or possibly even mediate to some degree.

4. *If available, pick someone whom your daughter also knows and trusts.* This type of person may have insights into your daughter and what might be going on with her, possibly being able to provide an alternative point of view.

5. *Seek professional guidance.* If you can get your daughter to join in the process of psychotherapy, all the better. But even if she won't, at this point or ever, you can benefit from a mental health professional trained to understand and help navigate through the complexities of relationship repair.

"At what juncture in this process should I seek assistance?", you might be wondering. The answer I'd say is, "When you believe you've tried many avenues and your daughter continues to resist or gives you some lip service, telling you all is okay, but the sassy behavior doesn't change." The kind of assistance you seek will depend upon your unique situation. This may entail an intervention like when Wendy enlisted Peter's support, or simply having a family friend or relative have lunch with your daughter to get a better sense of her perspective.

Ideally, if you have a significant other who can be instrumental in moving the process along, please enlist their services. You're not asking your partner to take sides but to voice your pain to your daughter and encourage her to join in on the healing path. If you're divorced and have been one of the fortunate ones to have enjoyed a healthy co-parenting relationship with your ex, then they may also be a worthy team player. Just be careful, though, to make sure the person you enlist does not have a strained relationship with your daughter, especially if that someone is a new—stepparent.

Also be careful if you have other children whom you may want involved. It's not a complete rule-out. Just make sure you're not placing too much pressure on the sibling.

If it turns out you think long and hard and continue to have trouble imagining that there is anyone out there to understand your situation, let alone someone to help you, don't give up yet. You might be surprised how many other moms have been in your shoes and who might be willing to help, especially if you ask directly with great specificity of what you need.

Also, keep in mind, your goal is not to drag someone into the middle of your battle, and certainly not to get someone to take your side. Rather, your aim should be to gather support either through making direct contact with your daughter on your behalf to jump start the process, or simply to be the rock for you. And if no one will step in, don't worry. You've got this, mama!

CHAPTER 14

This Just Isn't Working

As the saying goes, "We can lead a horse to water, but we cannot make him drink." So is true in relation to our adult-to-adult relationships. Without sounding like a broken record, though sometimes we do need to hear a message repeated for it to sink in, we only have control and responsibility for our own behaviors, feelings, and their consequences. Our power resides within ourselves. You can neither control, nor should you attempt to take responsibility for, another independent adult's life and how they choose to live it. Therefore, as much as you may have tried to give the gift of love to your daughter along the way, offering amends, seeking forgiveness, setting new healthy boundaries, and inviting her to join the repair journey with you, she just may not be ready. And the hardest reality of all; she may *never* be ready. And that's not your fault.

For whatever her reasons, she may not embrace, let alone trust, being on a healing journey. She may not even believe it's possible. Even if she has been victimized to some degree in her life, if she doesn't see her own responsibility in healing from the past, she may stay mired in victim mentality forever; no matter what you do to try to assuage her doubts. While I believe anyone can learn to thrive if they choose, not everyone is always willing to undertake the challenge of transforming from victim to survivor mode and, ultimately, into thriver mode. It's also possible that your daughter suffers from some sort of serious mental health issue and refuses treatment, perceiving that everyone else is responsible for her suffering. Or maybe she has been hijacked by an addiction and all your efforts to get her help have failed.

If this reflects your situation, my heart goes out to you. Nevertheless, please pause and take another moment to honor yourself for having embarked on this arduous challenge, maybe now with a greater lightness of being. If nothing else, you have grown internally and can have a more meaningful relationship with yourself. Also, you have hopefully gleaned a clearer sense of how your own background influenced your choices as an adult and mother, have forgiven yourself, come to accept and embrace your own limitations, and even gathered some insight into the ways in which you can make changes that will make your life more rewarding. Plus, much of what you gained can be applicable and generalizable to other relationships in your life, possibly with people who might be more receptive to engaging in a healing process.

Melinda's Journey:

Melinda, a sixty-something-year-old mother and grandmother, suffered many traumas in her life, including both her parents dying at early ages and dealing with a sibling with severe mental illness. She married and had one daughter, Pam. Her husband cheated on her multiple times, among many other betrayals, and she finally divorced him when Pam was six years old. Her ex qualified as a deadbeat dad, i.e., he failed to pay child support, let alone ever show up to see his daughter. Fortunately, Melinda had been left a small inheritance, enough to supplement the monies earned from her job.

Melinda struggled, to say the least, but she worked hard and doted on Pam as best she could with the little energy she had left at the end of the day. Despite her efforts at creating a loving home environment, her daughter turned to drugs and alcohol as a young teenager. Her addiction worsened over the years, despite multiple drug and alcohol treatment programs. In her early twenties she hooked up with a guy, also a drug user, who spent time in and out of prison, mostly for petty theft and drug possession charges. Together, they had two daughters, both of whom Melinda would take care of on and off while her daughter would make feeble attempts to clean up her act.

Melinda suffered terribly, often fearing that she would lose her daughter to death at any point. She spent years desperately trying to save and rescue Pam, but to no avail. At times she would have a glimmer of hope when Pam would sober up. During those brief moments, Melinda would dangle her olive branch, inviting her daughter to get real with her about the underlying sources of her pain that were driving her to turn back to drugs over and above anyone she claimed to love, especially her own children. But in the end, Pam continued to migrate back to substance abuse, to the point of no longer being able to care for her children.

Pam could be very kind and sweet to her mom during times of sobriety. However, when she was using, she treated her mom like a punching bag. At a certain point, Melinda drew the line in the sand. She told her daughter she could no longer take her hostility and vitriol and would not have her around unless her daughter sought the help she needed and maintained a drug and alcohol-free life. Pam continued to choose the drugs.

Fortunately, Pam's daughters were taken in by one of their relatives (on their dad's side) who cared for them until they reached adulthood. Melinda tried her best to maintain some relationship with her granddaughters, but at the time they seemed to turn on her as they had heard multiple stories about her being an unloving mother. While Melinda's heart was broken, she knew she could never compete with Pam's love for drugs and the resulting distortions in her perception of reality. Hence, with nothing left to give, Melinda chose to protect her own sanity (and safety) and distance herself completely from Pam and she kept an arm's distance from her granddaughters.

On a few rare occasions, Pam would call and leave a message. On special occasions, Melinda would send a note, card, or photo, sharing her love for her daughter but all the while sticking to her boundaries. Tragically, after about ten years of keeping her distance with strict boundaries, Melinda received a phone call informing her that her daughter had overdosed and died. Melinda sought my help to deal with her grief and overwhelming feelings of guilt.

As you can imagine, Melinda suffered a pain in her heart so deep she could not even describe it while she shared with me the intensity of the relationship she had endured with her daughter. Despite Pam's constant mistreatment of her mom, Melinda blamed herself for her daughter's final demise, believing that she should've had more stamina and kept her daughter closer in her world. It took months in our therapy for her to finally be able to hold onto the reminders of the chaos and turmoil her daughter had brought to her life and how much she'd tried to help her. Eventually, Melinda was able to accept that she truly had done all that was conceivably possible; and then some. Over time, she became more self-loving and forgiving and reasonably guilt free, accepting she had ultimately made the best decision for herself by letting go.

On a positive note, her granddaughters, who had recently become young adults themselves, became more curious about their grandmother and wanted to establish the beginnings of a closer relationship with Melinda. While Melinda was understandably skeptical at first as she feared she'd be opening a can of worms, through our sessions and her growing confidence in setting healthy boundaries, she began to soften and open herself up to a relationship with them, taking it a day at a time. Last I heard, she and her granddaughters were building a closer emotional bond, no longer tied to their mother.

How to Know When to Sever Ties?

This is another one of those questions that I wish I could answer definitively, yet I just can't. Everyone's life story is complicated, filled with so many nuances, that even if I were to be able to cover every possible combination of circumstances, I'd still be reluctant to give "if this-then that" advice. Nevertheless, I can offer these questions for you to consider. Plus, before you tackle this unbearably hard decision, I highly suggest you seek professional counseling.

1. Does your heart or gut tell you that there is no hope, but you just won't listen because you're too afraid to let go?
2. Does your daughter abuse you?
3. Have you offered every form of healing given the resources available to you?
4. Have you tried asking her why she's either so mean to you or doesn't want anything to do with you?
5. Have you honored her boundaries (without violating them)?
6. Have you sought your own professional help?

If you answered "yes" to these questions, I'd say you probably have your answer: that it may be time to consider severing ties. However, if you still have some no answers, then maybe you try those avenues first before making that excruciating decision. You can also consider a temporary hiatus, letting your daughter know that you will always love her, but for now from afar. You can tell her your conditions and criteria for letting her back in but that you need the distance at this point. Of course, you may experience some guilt. But if so, remind yourself to save guilt for only those moments when you are doing something wrong. And regardless of what your own caregivers have taught you, there is nothing wrong with trying to protect and preserve your sanity, even if that means distancing yourself from the daughter whom you love so dearly. Remember, all stories don't end up like Melinda's. Your own strength in setting your limits lovingly and in enticing your daughter to join you on a new improved relationship journey might very well grant you the wish you desire.

Sugar and Spice Exercise:

Please take a moment to take a few deep breaths and give yourself a loving, meaningful hug. Pat yourself on the back, give yourself a high five, or whatever expression of gratitude registers best for you. You have done what most moms have never done for their daughters and it's unfortunate if your daughter cannot, or will not, embrace your efforts, but this should not be lost on you. Honor yourself and what you've accomplished. You're amazing!

CHAPTER 15

Enjoying Your New Gems

"Mother & Daughter"

"It's a special bond that spans the years. Through laughter, worry, smiles and tears. A sense of trust that can't be broken, A depth of love sometimes unspoken, A lifelong friendship built on sharing, Hugs and kisses, warmth and caring, Mother and daughter, their hearts as one-A link that can never be undone."

(Author, *Unknown*).

This certainly brought tears to my eyes. So sweet and such heart behind this message. I think we moms would all love to enjoy and cherish this experience with our daughters. And I hope more than anything that you and your daughter can find your path to this bonded connection forever. You've done all this work to make a safe space for her to heal with you. Naturally, you want to get to the place where you can take a breath and feel at ease knowing that you both want to create the yummiest of all mother—daughter bonds.

Practice patience. Just like learning a foreign language often comes with a lot of frustration and wondering whether you'll ever be able to put together a succinct and comprehensible sentence, let alone speak it with any ease, your relationship with your daughter may evolve more slowly than you would like it to and may involve a lot of practice, trial, and error. But unless your daughter downright refuses to re-open her heart, like a computer that crashes without any hope of repair, I'm pretty sure you'll see some positive results.

You were very brave. Please be proud of yourself. If or when the time is right, invite your daughter to possibly go through the exercises in the book in relation to her taking ownership of the ways in which she may have created discord or distance from you. She may not initially be receptive to this offering. But she might surprise you, especially if she's seen your own progress. No matter what, I invite you to honor yourself in all your efforts. Way to go, mom!

Sugar and Spice Exercise:

Now for the final sugar and spice exercise. Create a Mother-Daughter Appreciation Day for the two of you to honor your bond. Maybe you take a little trip together or just do something special in celebration of one another. I know we have Mother's Day, but I think we also need mother—daughter day. After all, everyone can use another holiday.

Whatever your version will be of this unique celebration, crystalize this with your daughter. Make it ceremonial. Focus on gratitude and the honoring of one another. Hey, you may even become an inspiration for other moms who have suffered heartache with their daughters.

And last but not least, I leave you with the following chant which Tiffany so beautifully shared with me from *The Book of*

Ho'oponopono: The Hawaiian Practice of Forgiveness and Healing (by Luc Bodin, M.D., Nathalie Bodin Lamboy, and Jean Graciet, Destiny Books, 2012)

Ho'oponopono:
I'm Sorry
Forgive Me
Thank You
I love You
With love and gratitude,
Dr. Debra

Addendum

Samples of Daughter's Answers to Six Questions

1. What do you wish your mother would have known about you during your teens, but you were afraid to ask/tell her? (e.g., you had an abortion, you tried a drug, you skipped school, etc.)
2. What are the top three emotional wounds you are still carrying around with you that you blame on your mom?
3. What can your mom do to heal these wounds?
4. What are the top three characteristics that annoy you most about your mom and wish she would change?
5. What are the top three things you cherish about your mom and hope will never change? (After all—moms need gratitude too!)
6. If you could name anything that you wish your mom would do for you now—what would it be? (On this one I ask you to please refrain from naming material objects for her to purchase for you and instead focus on what she can provide for you emotionally.)

From Felicity: mid-twenties

1. With an honest opinion, I never had to be afraid, but that's because I had an older sister. I knew the "yeses" and "no's" because I had watched the trials and tribulations of a teen trying to figure it out right in front of me. Another benefit of being the 2nd child was also I knew what not to ask. I knew the triggers that could potentially set my mother off. I actually think one of the best lessons I learned is transparency. People forget that our parents were also teens once. The more honest I was, the more I got out of my adolescence, being able to look my mother in the eye and say, "A guy I really like is going to be at this party tonight, can I go?" It made her understand my intention. The less I lied, the more I received.

   I remember telling my mom I had smoked weed for the first time and a friend's parent had found out while secretly going through her phone (bad idea and so uncool with no warrant). Her mom called me and said, "You have the weekend to tell your mom these four bad things you did." So, I told her, and my mom's immediate response was, "I'm a little caught off guard but thank you for telling me. So, did you like it?" Of course, she wasn't stoked and shared her opinions about it and why I was too young, but I was too afraid to tell her. Yet immediately I was relieved because my honesty was my saving grace. My friend's mom called her a few days later and she simply said, "I know, thank you for telling me, we're dealing with it on our own terms."

   The other instance was alcohol. Of course, I was a normal teen who drank and got way too drunk my freshman year of high school (learned my lesson and that vodka wasn't for me lol), and a few times after that, but again my reputation was to my mother. I was always careful and wanted to make her proud, so rebelling wasn't in my blood. BUT with being a child who never got in trouble, or at least caught 😉, when I came back from my first year at college, alcohol was free range. She knew that being strict about something I would be doing and had been doing for months when not under her roof wasn't worth the secrets. So, I didn't hide it. And I gained freedom because of it. I could go to a neighbor's house with a bottle of wine from our cabinets as long as I told her and kept her updated throughout the night.

So, to answer your question, my mom rarely told me no, but I worked hard on not giving her a reason to do so.

2. There's going to be way more than three but I'm just giving you extra to work with 🤪
   - A loaded question because I don't blame her. I blame my dad more than her by all means.
   - Without blame, I'm mad she wasn't around more but blame my dad because as a single mom she had to work every day to support us. I also wouldn't change a lot of the hurdles we were given because I wouldn't know Spanish if Daisy, my nanny, wasn't in my life. My empathy is derived from being thankful that we could deal with the circumstances we were given.
   - I blame her for not being able to find happiness in a relationship because she consistently chooses to put others first, my ultimate wound being that she continues to give at her own cost. This weighs on me because she is someone who consistently gives so much, then takes so little. And that has been passed down to me. As much as I am thankful that my mother instilled being kind and giving to others, I rarely put myself first. I'm told daily that I'm too nice, and it's a sacrifice for my own well-being and I see it in her every day.

Everyone else's happiness is important, but at what cost when your own is always shelfed?

- I love and hate the weight that was put on my shoulders to be the person she wanted me to be because she didn't achieve her dreams. I should add for context that she may not have achieved her original life plan, but she did end up where she was meant to be, and everything happens for a reason. Being seven years younger than my sister, I saw a lot more and experienced a lot more pressure to be what she wanted me to be. I knew she gave up so much for me that not living up to her expectations just wouldn't be fair. Yet, again, I do partially blame my father for my mother having to put her dreams on hold to be the adult our family needed. The weight to achieve my dreams and hers was something I felt necessary. It wasn't an aspiration; it was a must. I knew I could do it. I couldn't be more thankful that my intent to make her proud drove me to be the best I could possibly be. I think one of the more beautiful aspects of our relationship is her dreams slowly became mine and that was our bonding hub. My passions were hers as well.
- Side note: Because I think it contributes, I think as kids we think goals are our parents' expectations. We feel like failures when we don't hit said goals, which causes us to rebel or hide, when in reality, "I hope you make honor roll," doesn't mean, "You better make honor roll." It just means they're rooting for us, but nobody's perfect. It's not an expectation. We're not letting anyone down. Parents are proud of us for effort not outcome.

3. To feel the need to be healed over decisions that had been made would be to categorize these moments as mistakes or regrets when in reality every single moment we had together is

the reason I am who I am. For me, it's not wounding as much as it is acknowledgment of the dedication of who I've become to make her proud. I didn't do any of it for just me, I did it for us.

Just say when you're proud. I often ask my mom, "Did I make you proud?" Or go out of my way to do things that would make her happy and get no acknowledgment in return. I know my sister and I would both enjoy and benefit for more comments like "job well done."

For me, you sacrificed so much for me, I'm good. It's time we made you the star of the show.

4. Where do I begin? 😂 In the best way possible, I'd say each of these to her face.
   - Patience. Somehow, I got an undeniable amount of patience and I get worried for people who see my mom's bad side. Though she means well, I would not want to be on her bad side. Yet, the older I've gotten the more I realize it's the fight or flight side of her that lives to protect. BUT I will say as a woman in 2022, a role model to say the least, gender has no effect on her, and she is the definition of letting nothing slip by.
   - Stubbornness. Times have changed and will continue to change. So instead of being so set in your ways, be able to adapt. Listen and at least try to understand before being so quick to say no. Sometimes when someone says, "You wouldn't understand.", it's because you're not taking the time to understand why you're in denial of a new future.
   - Continually putting others first. I would do anything for her to put the same effort she does into other people's happiness, and instead put it into her own.

5. What are the top three things you cherish about your mom and hope will never change? (After all, moms need gratitude too!)
   - Her sass and wit. In some other life my mom would have been a comedian for sure. Her one-liners are iconic. She's got Jane Fonda and Chelsea Handler vibes. We respect the blunt honesty, but even more so respect the audacity to challenge opinions when she's lived through it.
   - Her selflessness. I thank her forever for my heart.
   - Her determination. To be a single mother and to juggle as much as she does, and did, deserves every award in the book.
   - Her ability to welcome anyone with open arms. The number of people that she has let live in our home.

If you could name anything that you wish your mom would do for you now, what would it be? (On this one I ask you to please refrain from naming material objects for her to purchase for you and instead focus on what she can provide for you emotionally.)

- I would never go to material objects for a question like this. This is one thing I always hated about being from LA. Everyone would always assume we were rich or had crazy money and were snobs or mean. (Btw your point is 100% valid but I have a point that explains why I think this is a good point. It boggles my mind that ultimately a question like this would lead people to go material for something that resonates so much deeper.)

I've probably said this to you and will probably say it again but my least and most favorite backhanded compliment I got going to school in OR is, "You're too nice to be from LA." I am overly nice. But I also originally overcompensate for people around me who happen to have shorter fuses. So...

- I would ask to not feed the stigma. To be more patient, and kind.
- To relax. Take some deep breaths.
- To not take out frustrations on people who are just the messenger. A waiter, who has served the wrong food or if it's cold, a concierge at a hotel when a room or reservation is messed up. I understand being firm and getting what you expected and or asked for but to remember ultimately it had nothing to do with them personally. Get what you expected, but kill them with kindness, not fear.
- To acknowledge the struggles she has had over the years but to see that what she ultimately wanted to accomplish was accomplished. She can live her life without being stressed. Mission accomplished. She won. She completed single motherhood with flying colors. So, recognize it and be proud. She's getting older. I don't want her to think she still has to provide, and with that thinking she still needs to be glued to a desk.
- Lastly, to understand that as much as I will always be her mini me, I'm an adult now, and not every wish you had for me is going to come true. But if I'm happy then be happy!

Zena—early forties

1. I wish my mom asked how I was. I felt like she was very consumed with her own issues. I felt forgotten. I turned to my friends.
2. She had an affair, and I was asked to keep it a secret. She was emotionally neglectful during my childhood, and she could often be selfish.

3. She did apologize later on in life, which helped. I also wrote her a letter after my son was born telling her how I felt.
4. She can be selfish, entitled, and at times judgmental.
5. She's changed so much for the better. She's now caring, thoughtful, and very appreciative. We have a lot of fun together.
6. Luckily, she has provided me with what I need in my later years. It was the formative years that were the hardest.

Alicia—late thirties

1. What do you wish your mother would have known about you during your teens, but you were afraid to ask her? (e.g., you had an abortion, you tried a drug, you skipped school, etc.)

Honestly... secrecy, emotional repression, and sexual shame were so normal in our household that I avoided telling her as much as possible unless it was about an academic success, which I knew would be met with celebration. I was embarrassed to tell her when my period started. I was afraid to tell her if I'd fallen out with my friends. I was embarrassed to tell her when I started dating my first boyfriend. I bought a razor and shaved my legs for the first time when I was 13 without telling her. I didn't tell her when I started making love with my boyfriend. I didn't tell her I'd gone to the local family planning clinic to get the pill. (I was 15—I feel so much love and compassion for that brave inner child now!) I was never at all rebellious in terms of skipping school/staying out late/going to parties/taking illegal drugs, etc., so sex (and really, my whole process of puberty!) was the only big bone of contention between us.

2. What are the top three emotional wounds you are still carrying around with you that you blame on your mom?

Aww, bless her! 'Blame' seems a bit of a strong word. I'm grateful for all the conditioning she has shared with me, that I get to transmute this lifetime by bringing consciousness to it.

I think the biggest challenges are the deep sense of sexual shame, the inability to express my emotions for many years, and the belief that money is scarce and only comes through some kind of emotional dependency on a more powerful man.

3. What can your mom do to heal these wounds?

I don't think it is her responsibility to heal them. That's my work. Then, as I do the work, the healing ripples out and touches her, too. She listens to my process as best she can when it involves her, although she finds it very triggering to talk about anything that touches on our family skeletons in the closet. She is open to receiving my sharing by written message more than via in-person conversation, and I can honor that and not push her. I so clearly see her scared little inner girl and try to meet her with compassion where she is, giving myself the love and inner parenting that I wish she'd been able to give me, but know she couldn't and still can't. That's okay!

4. What are the top three characteristics that annoy you most about your mom and wish she would change?

Her pattern of over-giving and then becoming reactive and self-pitying when she has run out of energy. Her obsession with talking about her friend's grandchildren and the birds in the garden instead of her (and my!) childhood trauma used to bother me, but I have accepted it now. Her inability to express her emotions and needs clearly.

5. What are the top three things you cherish about your mom and hope will never change? (After all, moms need gratitude too!)

Her big, giving, generous heart. Her ability to make friendly small talk with strangers and make them feel very comfortable easily. How crap she is with technology and how it always makes us laugh at the start of video calls!

6. If you could name anything that you wish your mom would do for you now what would it be? (On this one—I ask you to please refrain from naming material objects for her to purchase for you and instead focus on what she can provide for you emotionally.)

I can't actually think of anything. I mean, it would be wonderful if we could sit down and have a mature, NVC-based conversation about both of our feelings about what happened when I was young, like I did with my father several times over the last couple of years before he died. But she doesn't have the tools and inner resources to do that, and I'm not going to push it on her. I'm grateful that she is at least somewhat open to hear my perspective by message, even if talking about it face to face is still too much.

Larissa—late thirties

1. I wish I could've spoken to her about my sexuality, my first boy kiss, my first girl kiss, how I got drunk for the first time and got a massive hickey from a girl. Homosexuality/bisexuality was and is very taboo in my culture so there really wasn't room for openness or acceptance. I wish I could have told her how scared I was all the time.

2. She knew I was a "sexual person" and craved intimacy and physical connection, but she never tried to help me understand it or develop safety with others. She shamed me and blamed me instead. "Save your virginity until marriage! Don't be a whore! Why are you dressed like a slut?" 1. I'm pretty sure she caught me masturbating and pretended like it never happened. 2. Having unsafe relationships with men, just like she had with my father. Since she wasn't able to keep herself or my brother and I safe from my alcoholic dad (and stayed married to him), I learned to devalue myself and date men who were either abusive or avoidant. I had no sense of self, no practical life skills, no relationship skills. I was left to my own vices and expected to figure everything out on my own. From relationships to academics, to financial matters. 3. Becoming a caretaker was my only value and it became my career path as well! Luckily, I've done a lot of work to heal and unblend from my dysfunctional past but being in a one-down position and only valuable if helping others/people-pleasing is a survival mechanism I learned to stay attached and loved by my mom.
3. I've accepted that I must heal these wounds myself and that she, unfortunately, isn't capable of doing so. I've made peace with it, have forgiven her, and do my best to be nonjudgmental and loving towards her. I've come to terms with the past and know that I can't really blame her because she wasn't treated with the love and compassion she needed as a child either.
4. I wish she wasn't so stubborn 2. Closed-minded 3. Grandiose.
5. Her vulnerability when she shows it 2. Her brilliant mind (before dementia) 3. Her devotion to family.
6. It's a hard question because she is so incapacitated that she's not able to do much, but what has happened is that she has softened the walls around her heart. She is gentler and more loving with me, and her continuing to do that is all I want.

From Sari—early thirties

1. I wish she knew how lonely and worthless I felt. Anytime I engaged in anything questionable she *always* found out. So, I can't give an example that is tangible. What I sense she didn't know, rather, was how much turmoil I was in on an inner emotional level. I am a highly sensitive individual, and this sensitivity made being at high school terribly unpleasant and difficult. I never felt like she attuned to this and looking back I wish I had dived into my talents at that age, such as writing and performing. I don't feel like my gifts were ever acknowledged. Instead, perseverations about all that I was doing which was *wrong* was. For example: dressing provocatively, wanting to engage in discourse on controversial subject matters, etc.
2. The top three emotional wounds would be: 1. Lack of attunement (my mother wasn't a safe person back then. To this day, if I share something vulnerable with her, she will later throw it back at me and attack me for it). This lack of attunement I was perpetually experiencing with her affected my love map to be magnetically drawn to men with narcissistic traits. In these dynamics I feel the familiar and similar loneliness and "unseen" wounds which developed through my relationship with my mother. 2. Always being told growing up that things I wanted were "too expensive." Further corroborating this was constant joking out at dinners that I needed to 'order off of the children's menu' even when I was in my late teens. Just a couple of years ago I met someone on a date at a restaurant where the cheapest salad was over $30. The main courses were $50+. I felt incredible anxiety, ordering only a salad and still feeling guilty about it. My anxiety would have been waylaid if I had ordered a glass of wine to calm my nerves. However, even that felt scary (even though he encouraged me to get a drink if I

wanted while saying he didn't drink). I resorted to lemonade. Growing up, whenever a guest ordered an alcoholic beverage or a coffee at the end of the meal, etc., they were later gossiped about as having gall. I am still working through the wounds of feeling worthy and deserving of being treated well and having nice things. 3. Shame and the inability to be outspokenly prideful about my work. Whenever I put something out into the world my mother would attack it as not being in alignment with her values and beliefs. This is one wound where I feel I have made a lot of progress, but it is a constant battle.

3. My mother needs a trauma informed therapist where she can work out all of the abuse she endured as a daughter. I don't think she has ever done that. And so, her wounds are passed down to me. I know she is currently seeing a therapist once a month and it doesn't sound like the therapist is trauma informed. She's out in North Carolina and focuses on "eating plans" because my mother has an overeating disorder. I could go on and on about activities my mother could do to help herself become more whole… but it's not really my place. I think words she could say that would help soothe where my own pain and trauma live in my body would be something like, "I'm sorry I wasn't able to encourage and validate your talents and experiences. Please understand my mother didn't do that for me. She would attack my artistry and it's something I gave up before I ever had you. So, it's really hard for me to see you in the ways you want to be seen by me because I never got that from my mother." Something to the effect which would reveal that she is more aware of her own shadows and how they affect those around her would feel incredibly grounding and soothing.
4. Top three characteristics which annoy me about my mom, and I wish she would change: 1. Her projections. She has several people in her sphere who she complains about being "so

competitive" and she goes on to say, "I'm just not a competitive person." She represses and denies her own competitive nature and thus casts characters in her world to hold the projection for her. 2. Her perseverations on gossip. I would love to engage in more philosophical and spiritual conversations with her, but I don't feel met in these interests and instead the common ground is to talk about other people. 3. Her need to keep everyone happy and entertained all of the time. I think if she would surrender a bit more and invest on a trip that's not through a travel company for once and instead a spiritual healing retreat for women, her entire nervous system would shift to being more regulated.

5. 1. Her willingness to talk with me whenever I need her.
   2. Her abundance of food and her desire for adventure. She always asks what I would like before I come to visit and makes sure her kitchen is stocked full of my desired foods and drinks. Additionally, her perseverance with food lends itself to multiple and constant meals out which are often interwoven with some fun adventures or escapades.
   3. Her humor. She is able to laugh at people's idiosyncrasies and make jokes about the most innocuous of occurrences. Sometimes when I'm emotional and lamenting to her about something someone said, she will burst out laughing. I appreciate this because it allows me to soften and see the humor in things I sometimes take too seriously.
6. I am sort of breaking your rule here in this answer, but it is my most honest answer. Currently, I am not speaking with my mother. She shared with me a year ago that my grandpa gave four million dollars to her and her sister. All throughout my life my mom has talked about my grandpa's money to me and has shared that I am receiving 5% in the will. My grandpa decided to give some money away early, and I can't help but assume he thought

his daughters would share with their children. I know that when my great grandmother died, she left an inheritance to my grandma who then sponsored my mother's master's degree. I just find it so unloving, cold, and selfish that my mom is not sharing the tiniest percentage with me especially when she's already a millionaire and married to a wealthy, retired engineer. While I am trying to start my own business, and a nonprofit, and pay excruciating rent and cost of living expenses in LA. I've had numerous conversations with her about this over the past year, and she remains rigid. It has caused me to lose sleep and sent me into a spiral of falling for scams to try and make up for money I believe should be mine. This may sound like a lot of blame and victim consciousness. And I sense the only way to break free from that consciousness is to distance myself from any communication with her for a long time. If she came forward and offered me a financial gift (I would *never* even desire this from her or expect it from her. But because I know she just received millions from my grandpa, and I've had details shared with me about finances, this is why it is my answer.) It would feel like reparations for the psychological, physical, and emotional abuse I received from her as a child. And it doesn't need to be "reparations", either. Just a generous check saying, "Hey, I see you working hard to realize your dreams. I know starting a business is expensive, as is LA. Keep making the world a brighter place, here you go." Anything to that effect would feel like potent balm to wounds which still feel a bit gaping and bloody.

Naomi—early 30s

1. That I punched a boy at school in the testis and I was so afraid of the consequences I cried nearly all night but could not tell my mum.

2. That I have problems trusting someone (also close ones).
3. We are all very independent women in my mum's family but have problems trusting men.
4. We love to sweep things under the rug. I would wish to blame this on her, but I am very much aware that I am responsible for dealing with this.
5. I wished she would talk to me more openly.
6. That she endures a lot when it is actually too much for her. She could communicate much earlier. Then she reaches a point where she explodes.
7. The needier someone is, the more she cares. My brother who is in his 30s gets much more time and attention from her. I assume it is because I am much more independent. I wished she would not encourage his neediness with her behavior.
8. Her independence, her readiness to help others, and her zest for action.
9. Listen to me, ask me honestly how I am. She only told me in my 20s that my dad is not my biological dad, and this caused a big trust issue in our very good relationship that is still not completely solved. I would love her to work with me on that — in addition to the work I do on myself here.